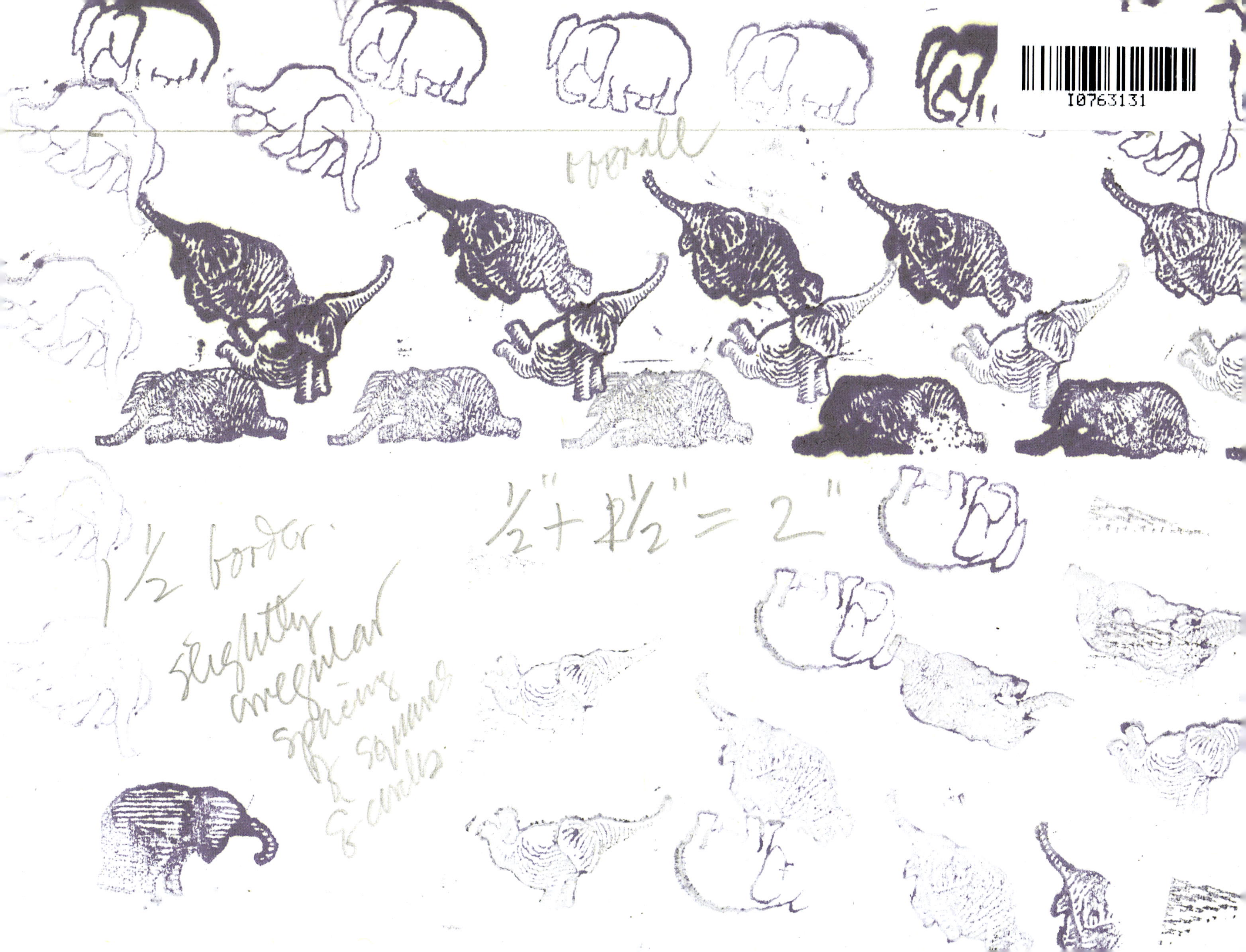

overall
1/2 border
1/2" + 1 1/2" = 2"
slightly irregular spacing & squares & circles

ELEPHANT HOUSE

or, The Home of Edward Gorey

photographs and text by Kevin McDermott

with illustrations by Edward Gorey

foreword by John Updike

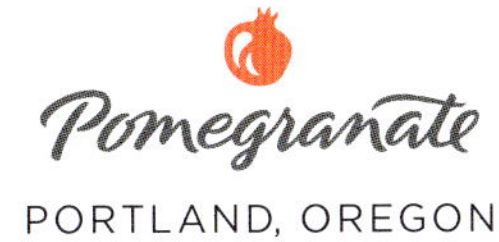

PORTLAND, OREGON

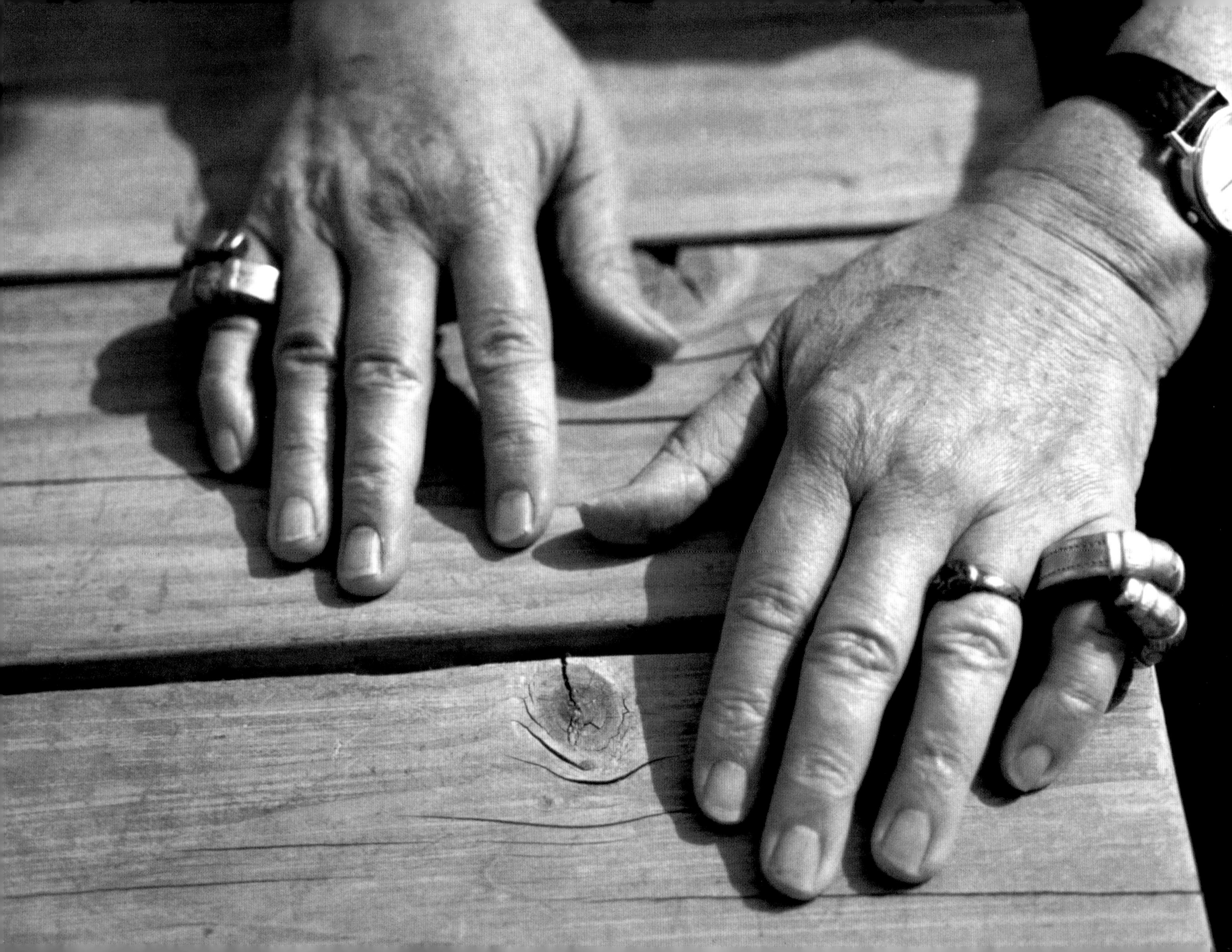

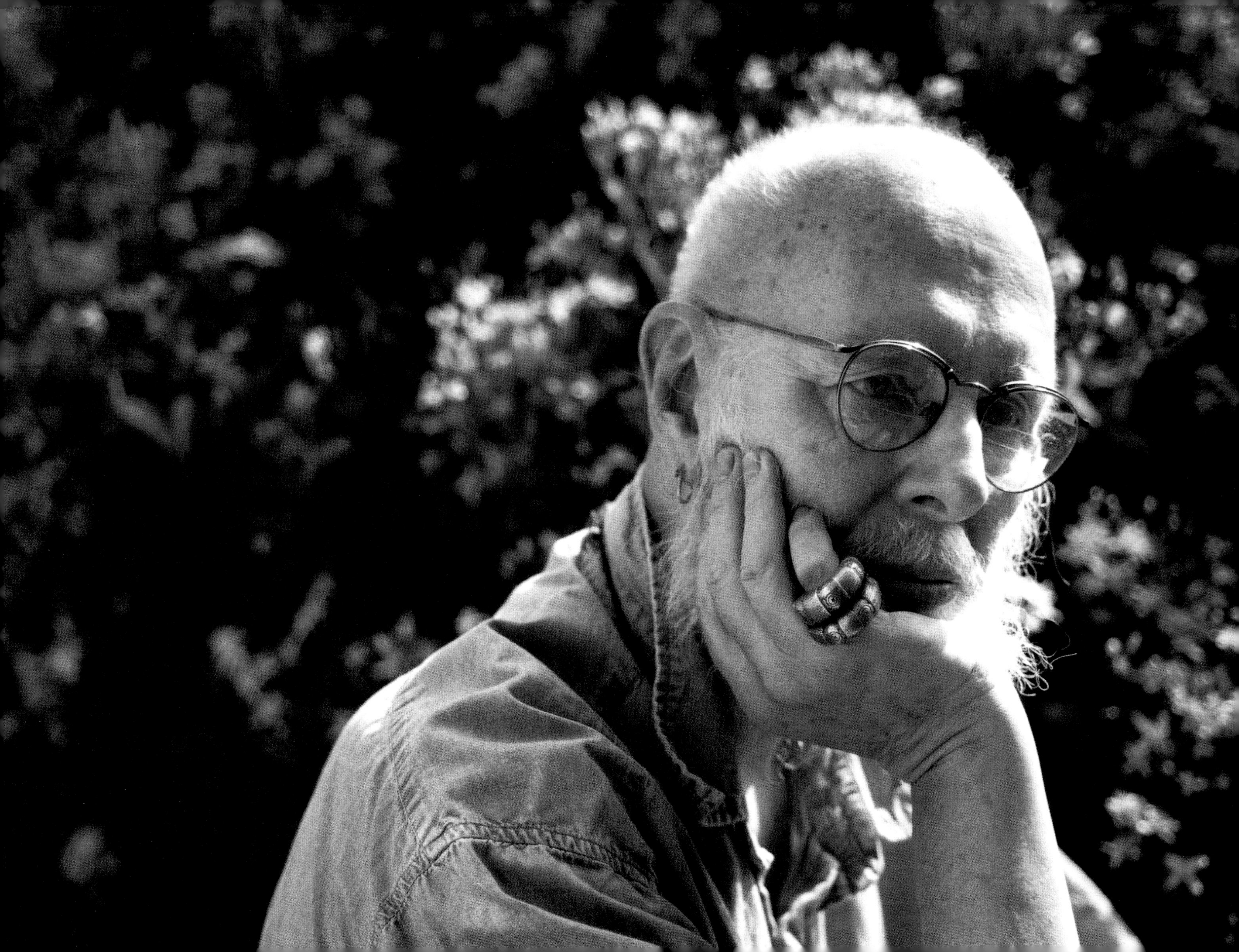

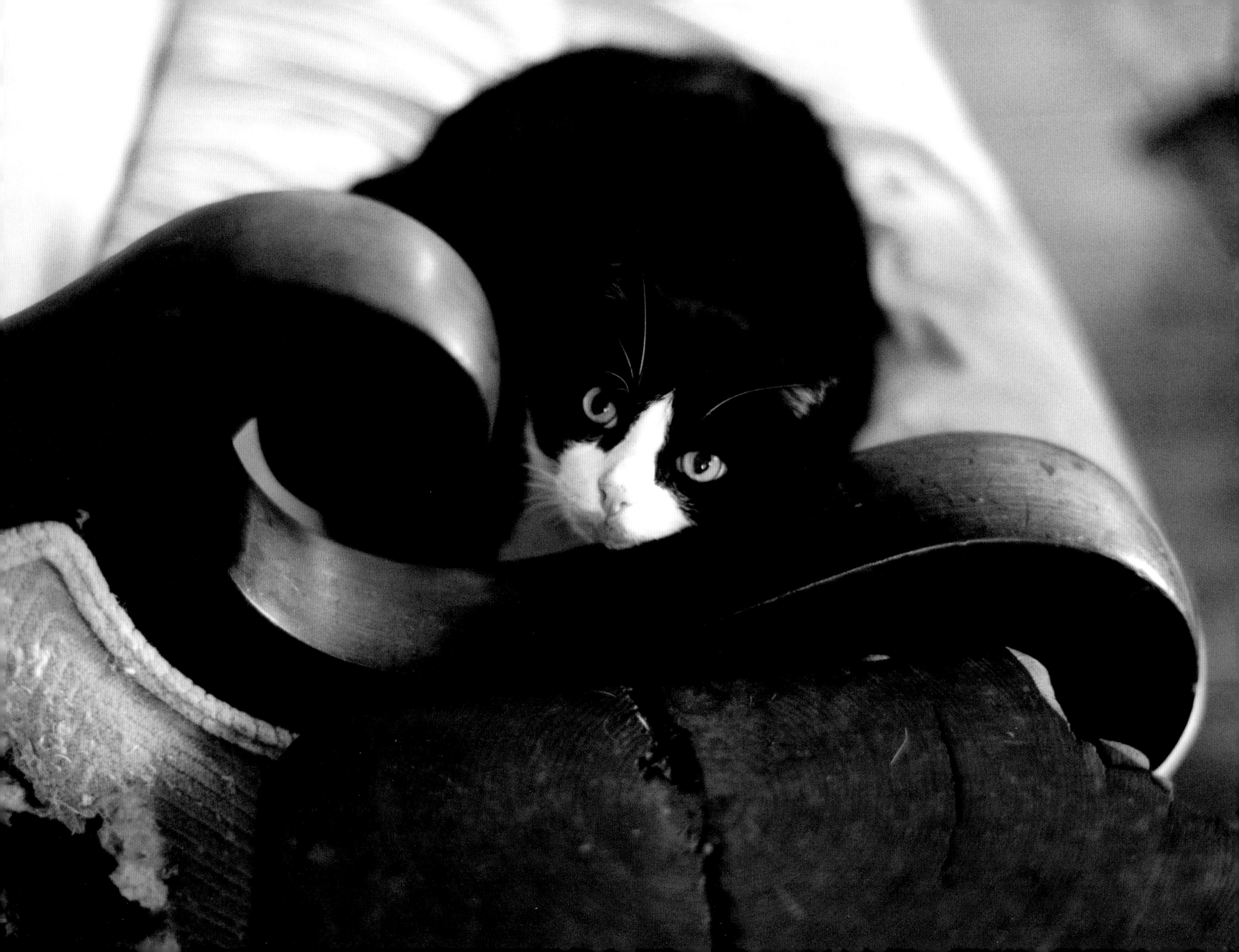

FOREWORD

Edward Gorey was, artistically speaking, a thin man who cast a fat shadow. His books, all of them slender and most of them distinctly whimsical, inspired an enthusiasm and loyalty disproportionate to their size. Edmund Wilson, no less, became a Gorey fan and collector, and in a lengthy *New Yorker* review admired how Gorey "has created a whole little personal world, equally amusing and somber, nostalgic and claustrophobic, at the same time poetic and poisoned." Gorey came to my own attention when I entered Harvard in the fall of 1950: the Registration issue of *The Harvard Advocate,* the college literary magazine, sported a cover drawn by "Edward St. J. Gorey" that showed, startlingly, two browless, mustachioed, long-footed, high-collared, seemingly Edwardian gentlemen tossing sticks at two smiling though disembodied jesters' heads. The previous term's Commencement issue, also made available to incoming freshmen, displayed a virtually identical pair of bizarrely profiled male persons, this time waving "L'adieu," with white handkerchiefs and akimbo feet, to what appeared to be an Arctic sun. The style was eccentric but consummately mature; it hardly changed during the next fifty years, as I followed it on Anchor Books (the pioneering quality paperback line, with many covers drawn and lettered by Gorey), through a hail of playbills and precious chapbooks, to its belated arrival in the pages of *The New Yorker* and its superb animated version in the opening titles of WGBH's *Mystery!* television program. An artist and a writer who never strayed from his curious, carefully crosshatched corner of sinister nostalgia, Gorey wound up widely on view.

Like another Edward—Lear—he was a cheerfully morbid bachelor uncle who refused the injunction of St. Paul to put away childish things. His hobbies, from the ballet of Ballanchine to antique-store gleanings, were pursued with a vocational thoroughness—indeed, his life was virtually all hobby. These photographs of Gorey's home, taken a week after his sudden death at the age of seventy-five, show a master collector, an acquisitor of appealing oddments who in his solitude filled room after room with inanimate friends—dolls and stones and tomes and metal frogs and tinted glass and lead sinkers and marble eggs and TV tapes and simulacra of elephants. Then there were the living cats, occasionally dabbling in wet ink as Gorey labored at his tiny work table, and the big old wooden house itself; New Englanders will recognize the peeling sills, the loosening panes, the pine floorboards, the semi-abandoned air. Wood deteriorates but can always be renewed and replaced; such houses prompt a spirit of improvisation, and this spirit lingers here, embodied in an endless collection of cherished things. Kevin McDermott's photographs bring us closer to Gorey than his art, in a way; the art evoked a unique bygone world he and we could escape to, where patient crosshatching deepened wistful shadows and the shy personae never looked us in the eye. Gorey the householder feels like a happier man, who threw nothing out, and kept the pleasure in everything. The odd miniature worlds of his books were ones he somehow wanted to inhabit; here is the world, equally personal and creative, that he did inhabit.

John Updike

PREFACE

I met Edward Gorey in 1985, on my twenty-first birthday. On that rainy winter night, I waited with about thirty other young acting students in the corner of a dance studio; a group of six men sat behind a long table. Suddenly a pianist began playing the tango "La Cumparsita," and we moved diagonally across the floor, our arms up in an Egyptian stance. Our palms faced the ceiling, our knees were slightly bent with our center of gravity thrown back and off balance, and our faces pointed up at a forty-five-degree angle as we looked directly into the track lights. With a combination of deathly seriousness and total nonchalance we moved across the floor. Huge gulps of laughter filled the room. Sounding like a cross between a large gull and a hyena, it was coming from behind the table. I had never heard anything like it. It was Edward Gorey's giant, infectious laugh.

As I listened to Edward laugh, and my friends and soon-to-be friends moved across the floor in this Goreyesque manner, I knew I wanted to be part of this world. It was an audition for a production soon to be called *Tinned Lettuce: or The New Musical*. I was a drama student at New York University and one of the lucky nineteen selected to be in the cast. We spent the next six weeks rehearsing with Edward and our director, Daniel Levans. I had a great time creating such Gorey characters as "The Enraged Telephone" and "The Frozen Man" from unpublished stories. Over the next fifteen years, I performed in many productions of Edward's works. (Several years after *Tinned Lettuce*, the production evolved into *Amphigorey: the Musical* with performances in Philadelphia and Cambridge, and in 1994 I became the producer of its off-Broadway production.) By the spring of 1995, however, I had decided to give up acting and I moved from New York to Cleveland, reinventing myself as a graphic designer and photographer. Early in 1999 I received a call from the artistic director of Provincetown Repertory Theatre to once again participate in a Gorey theatrical production. I was not certain I wanted to spend a summer in Provincetown, Massachusetts, and risk losing my clients in Cleveland. With a little coaxing I agreed to go. Due to a last-minute contract dispute with another actor, I was promoted to the role of the play's narrator/author—in effect playing Edward. I was uneasy with this change. I had prepared myself for the roles I had played for more than a decade, most notably the deranged opera fan Jasper Ankle in *The Blue Aspic*. I had also looked forward to spending my days at the beach, not indoors memorizing lines. Taking on the role of the author was a lot of responsibility. Again, some coaxing took place. In the end I had needed to do little memorization. When we started rehearsing, I realized that I had heard Edward's stories for so many years (in rehearsals and productions) that they were now part of me.

Because I had known and respected Edward and his work for so long, I was interested in his reaction to my new role. He did not participate in the production and did not attend any rehearsals, but on opening night he made the forty-five-minute drive from his home in Yarmouthport to Provincetown. I heard that huge, unique laugh. I was pleased and relieved when he came back to the theater for many performances, often inviting friends. I visited Edward several times during that summer discussing the idea of bringing this production (then called *Amphoragorey*, with music by Peter Matz) to New York. He was very enthusiastic, encouraging me to retain my role in the play. In the autumn of 2001 we did succeed in producing the play in New York as *The Gorey Details*.

On April 15, 2000, the phone rang. I was told that Edward had just died. It was a shock. Over the next few days I was informed of the estate's plan to go to Edward's house to secure the property. It would be necessary to remove valuable art and other objects from the house immediately and then begin the arduous task of sorting through the massive accumulation of Gorey's life. I asked the estate if I could photograph the house. I realized the uniqueness of Edward's home would soon be gone and that it needed to be preserved in some way. The Gorey estate agreed. This also gave me a personal and meaningful way to say farewell to someone who had been so

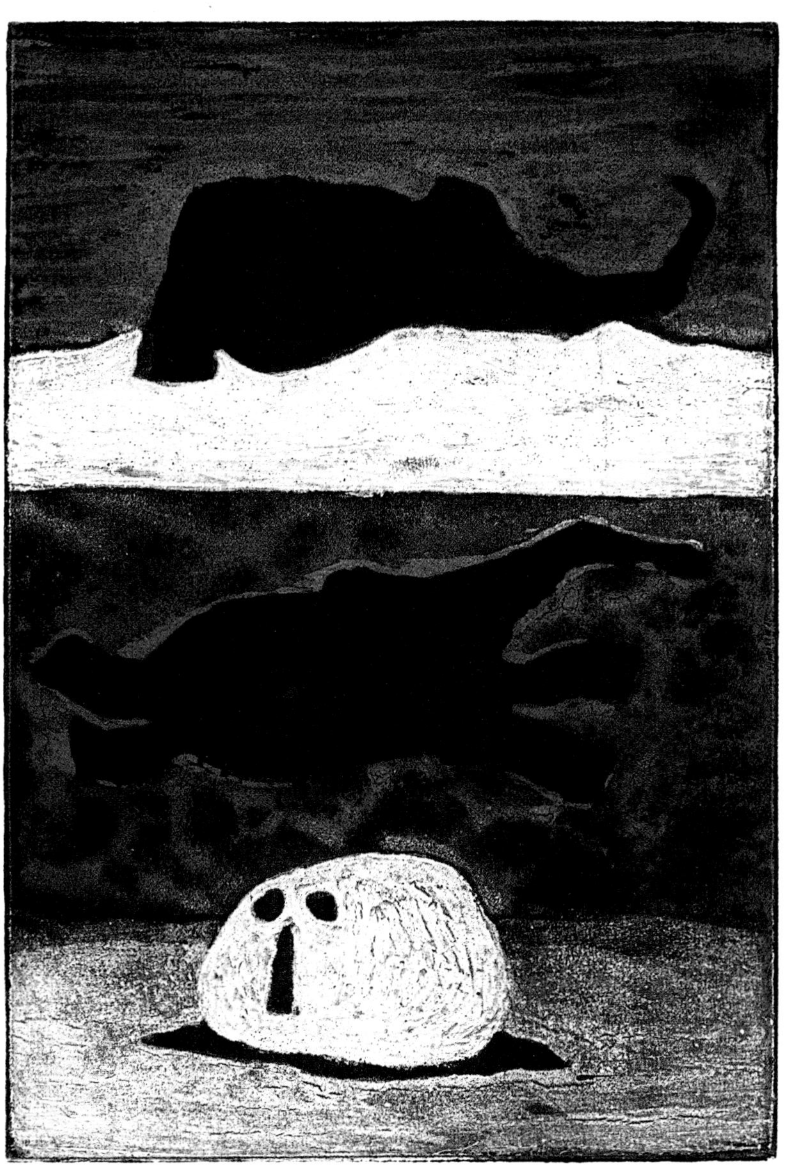

generous to me. On Friday, April 21, I drove to the Cape. The next morning, a week after Edward died, I photographed the house.

After Edward's death I learned that he had given his great bulky home a special name known only to a few people: Elephant House. Why Elephant House? Perhaps it was inspired by the size of the house, or the exterior wooden shingles, which for many years were gray and crackled like elephant skin. Yet it seems a more whimsical explanation is the most likely. When Edward first toured the interior of the house he discovered, in an upstairs bathroom, an antique white porcelain toilet shaped very much like an elephant. In typical Edward fashion, he had the bathroom removed but saved the toilet, later incorporating it into the design of an end table.

Under the terms of Edward's will, Elephant House was placed on the market. It was purchased by a Massachusetts foundation with the announced intention to create a museum in honor of Gorey's artistic achievements and his contributions to the Cape community. In the summer of 2002, the Edward Gorey House was opened to the public. The museum also recognizes Edward's dedication to animal welfare. Edward had left his estate to the Edward Gorey Charitable Trust, which was established for the same purpose, consistent with his Taoist beliefs.

I hope these photographs convey a sense of Elephant House, the home where Edward lived happily and worked so industriously.

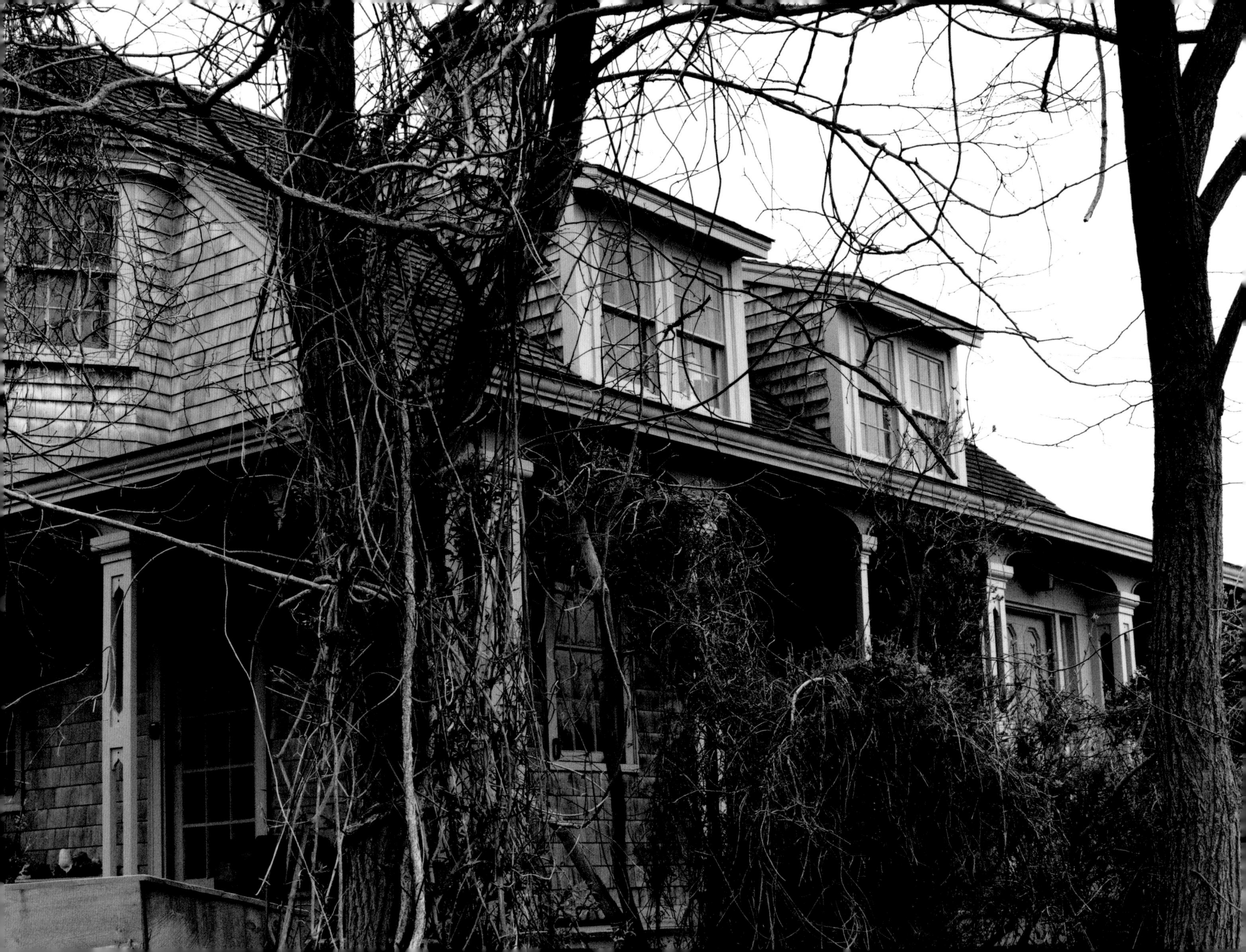

THE HOUSE

I was running a little late as usual. I pulled around the common and saw Edward sitting on a bench reading and waiting for me. I apologized as I parked my little red pickup truck in front of his house. He didn't seem put out in the least. There he stood, bearded, his tall lanky frame in a faded blue cotton button-down shirt, khaki shorts, and his usual white sneakers. It was August, and the day was bright. I couldn't help but notice the contrast of my tan, acquired from a summer in nearby Provincetown, with Edward's lack of tan from a summer spent in his studio in Yarmouthport. "Ooh, I have a great place to go to lunch," Edward said enthusiastically. "They sometimes have someone play the piano. And it's a hoot!"

"Sounds great," I said, anticipating Edward's comments on the choice of songs we were about to hear.

"But, before we go, I want to show you something." Edward led the way at a rather fast clip for a man of seventy-four. We hurried past the overgrown bushes in front of the house, and past the wooden deck and stairs which were covered with rocks of various sizes and shapes, to the lawn on the south side of the house. He gestured to the sloping hill that led to his barn behind the house. I searched the barn in the distance for some distinct eccentricity. We walked a few more steps. "No, not up there! Look, at your feet!" There, partially buried in the green grass, a few inches in front of my sneakers, was a rock. It was about six inches in diameter, and a few inches away was another rock of about the same size. The curving line of these rocks made its way up the hill, stretching on for about fifteen feet. "It's my serpent," Edward said.

"I love it. It's too bad it's so low to the ground. Once the grass grows tall, no one will see it. It will disappear."

"Precisely," Edward said. "It's waiting to be discovered."

The house at 8 Strawberry Lane in Yarmouthport, Massachusetts, was built in the early nineteenth century as a Federal-style full Cape. Constructed by Captain Edmund Hawes, the house is located on the eastern side of the horseshoe road bordering the Yarmouthport common. The common is a one-acre parklike setting facing on the Old King's Highway (the coach road, now Route 6A). From the outset, local residents used the common area to manufacture bricks for the construction of their homes. Around 1850, it was leveled and planted with ornamental trees. After Captain Hawes was lost to the Atlantic Ocean, the house was acquired by Nathaniel S. Simkins, who made improvements by adding rooms, a stick porch, a Federal window, and several dormers. It was a Federal Cape no more. The house stayed in the Simpkins family for generations, eventually becoming only a summer residence before falling into disrepair. It was finally offered for sale in the late 1970s.

After graduating from Harvard University in 1950, Edward Gorey began visiting relatives on Cape Cod, first sharing a small cottage at the edge of a marsh on Freezer Road in Barnstable, then, in 1963, a larger house nearby on Mill Way. He spent the rest of his time in New York City, living in a Victorian brownstone studio apartment on East 38th Street near Madison Avenue, where he had moved in 1953 to work in the art department at Doubleday & Company.

Eventually, the attic at Mill Way, with its view of Barnstable harbor, became Edward's summer residence. Edward was a devotee of the choreographer George Balanchine, and would not leave Manhattan until Balanchine's New York City Ballet season ended in July. He would then drive to the Cape, often with his friends Mel and Alex (Alexandra) Schierman. Alex had met Edward while she was ushering at New York City Ballet performances at City Center. They quickly discovered other mutual interests including film and the Beatles (on the drive up to the Cape, Alex and Edward enjoyed passing the time singing Beatles songs).

The house on Mill Way was the summer home for Edward and various family members—Edward's cousins Eleanor and Elizabeth ("Skee"); their father and mother, Benjamin and Betty Garvey; Skee's husband, Roy Morton, and their young son Kenneth—as well as others. A favorite pastime was searching local antique shops and yard sales with Eleanor and Skee for items to furnish Mill Way. (Eleanor, Skee, and Edward were the inspiration for his book *The Deranged Cousins.*)

In 1979, while driving along Route 6A in Yarmouthport with Mel and Alex, Edward saw a For Sale sign on the neglected 8 Strawberry Lane property. After parking the car, the three proceeded to examine the closed house through the windows. In one of Edward's many small pocket journals, July 1979 entries record his first thoughts about his future residence: "bookcases conflict with heating?"; "new fireplace for kitchen?"; "vines up porch and fence maybe?"; "coloured front door/or resist?" There are no written concerns regarding practical matters such as the soundness of the plumbing or of the roof. The rundown condition did not concern Edward. He had a hit play on Broadway *(Dracula)*, and for the first time in his life he had substantial personal income—he wanted this to be his first house. He made no inquiry about the structural stability of the house; he simply asked, "How much?"

Soon Edward owned the house, but it would be another six years before he would actually sleep there. He continued to live at Mill Way while making improvements to his new property. The first winter, while friends and family were away, he hired a contractor and set to work remodeling the interior. He tore down walls to open up rooms, and he removed two bathrooms. When the first round of renovations was completed, the contractor informed Edward that the roof needed to be replaced. The cost however was too much for Edward's budget; several years would pass before he was able to afford a new roof. By then, water had damaged some of the interior work he had done.

Edward loved animals—all living creatures—and he usually let them share the house. During the early phase of renovations, before Edward moved in, Mel and Alex and their two children stayed at the house for several summers. Throughout the night, they could hear the scratching and clawing of a colony of raccoons that lived in the crawl space below the house and in the attic. The raccoons stayed until the arrival of a skunk forced their removal.

In 1983, Edward lost his apartment in New York, and with the death of Balanchine, he had little reason to return to the city. At last, in the autumn of 1986, he made the move from Mill Way to Elephant House. Edward now had a home of his own, or at least one shared only with his cats.

Despite seven years of renovations, the exterior of the house was still in poor shape. Windows were broken; many of the gray shingles, which hadn't been painted in years, were chipped and cracked; and the grounds surrounding the house were substantially overgrown. Some supportive friends felt that this situation was appropriately "Goreyesque." Edward talked about "fixing up the place."

Finally in 1995, with his finances improving, Edward repaired the windows, reshingled the house, and replaced the roof. As with most matters pertaining to the house, he followed his own unorthodox methods. It rarely bothered him if those methods yielded something other than conventional progress. When he began the second round of renovations he hired a painter to paint the exterior of the house. The painter asked for a down payment. Edward asked what the total fee for the work would be. He was told $12,000. Edward wrote a check for the full amount. The painter worked for a short time and then disappeared. When asked why he had given the painter all of the money in advance, Edward replied, "It seemed easier that way."

Edward also became interested in gardening. He had always been proud of the house's existing plantings, including a huge and rare southern magnolia tree that flourished on its protected south side. Two large overgrown boxwoods, said to be over one hundred years old, stood at the front of the house like unruly shields guarding against the outside world. Wild clematis grew along the north side of the house. When viewed from the main road, the vines seemed to devour the house. They bloomed in September and October, and when they did, they were radiant.

But the boxwood and clematis had come with the house. What Edward could cultivate on his own was a different story. With his newfound interest in gardening, he was delighted when a friend called to tell him she had discovered a Cape nursery that carried black pansies. The very existence of black flowers amused him. Edward promptly bought all they had. He requested help from his friend Rick Jones, regarding the appropriate way to plant them. Edward stood on the porch as Rick took a flower, dug a small hole, and planted it. Edward watched intently, then asked Rick to plant another. Then another. Soon Edward went back into the house, and Rick planted all the pansies.

For many years Edward drove a bright yellow Volkswagen Beetle, miraculously folding his six-foot-three-inch frame into the driver's seat. He was so fond of the car that he drove it until it would drive no more. The car, parked in front of 8 Strawberry Lane, was a well-known sight, with its OGDRED license plates (a pen name Edward used for more than one of his early books). It was replaced with a black Volkswagen Golf. Although good behind the wheel, Edward had little interest in the maintenance of his car. On one occasion Rick received a distress call from Edward: "I can't make my car go." Rick expected to find engine trouble. However, when he arrived he discovered that Edward had tried to drive over a mound of gravel. With none of its four wheels touching the ground, the car was stuck on the top of the mound. Rick returned home to get a shovel. While Edward remained in the car, Rick shoveled until it was safely on the ground.

On most Saturdays Edward and his cousins used the car to visit antique shops and yard sales. As with his house, the car amassed its own accumulation of found objects, including stuffed animals and other creatures, arranged across the dashboard, on the back seat, and on the car floor. Mingled with this menagerie was an extensive selection of cassettes and eventually CDs. During the summer—Gorey theater time—costumes, puppets, and props also inhabited the small car. It was a challenge to find a place to sit.

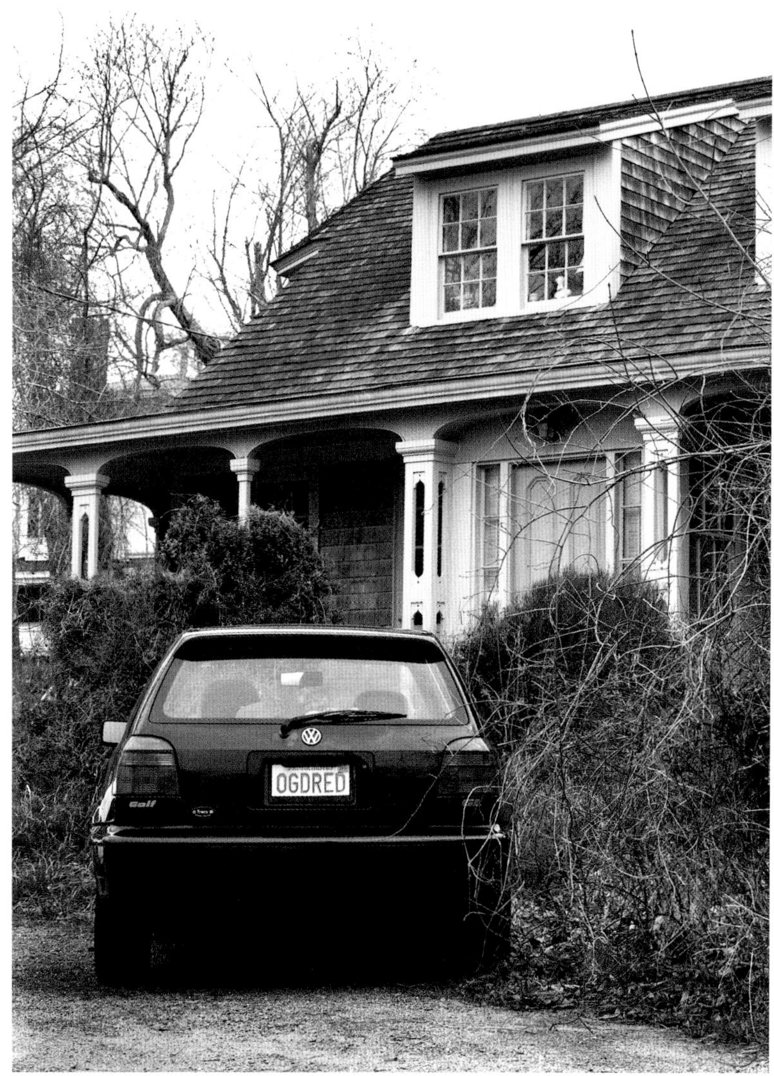

A young man grew increasingly peaky
In a house where the hinges were squeaky.
   The ferns curled up brown,
   The ceilings flaked down,
And all of the faucets were leaky.

—Edward Gorey, from *The Listing Attic*

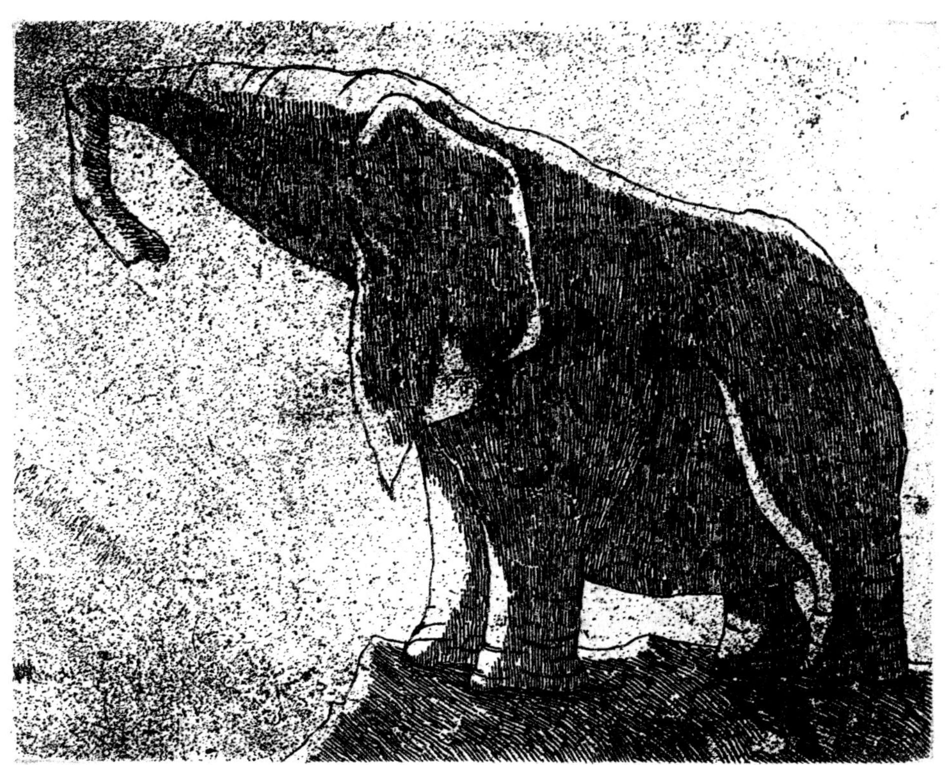

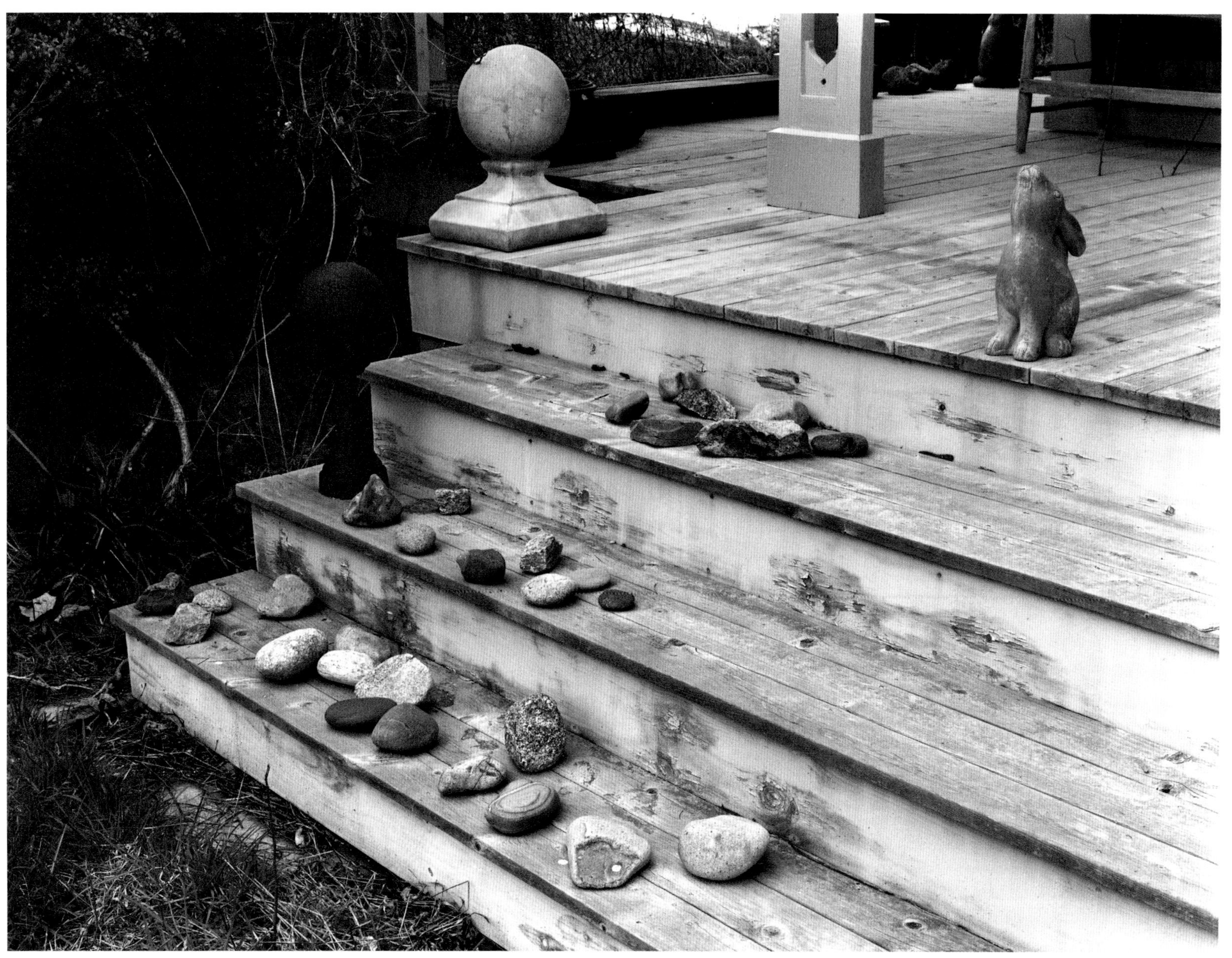

The Porch

After running the obstacle course of overgrown bushes, hedges, and dangling vines along the path on the north side of the house, one would arrive at the porch steps. Edward loved to "arrange" things. He liked to bestow relationships on a group of objects, raising juxtaposition to a new level of insight and eccentricity. From the moment you entered his property you might find yourself standing "in" one of his arrangements. A "family" of miscellaneous flatirons marched around the corner of the house. A bird's nest rested on the treadle of an antique sewing machine. Rocks of various sizes and shapes could resemble frogs if viewed from a certain angle, or for a brief time of day with the appropriate light and shadow. Edward often explored the shorelines of the Cape for important rocks. A rock in which he discerned the shape of a frog delighted him. He could find a hidden image in a variety of objects: pliers became dragons, shears were birds in flight, remnants of an unidentified machine could be a four-legged cousin to the Wuggly Ump. Sometimes the newfound object remained a puzzle until Edward placed it appropriately with previously found objects, and in some way its mystery would be revealed. Discovery was an important component of Edward's collecting, and this joy of discovery permeates his work.

Birds had built a nest over the light at the front porch door. Edward would never think of removing the nest; he simply did not use that door. The nest remained for the last years of Edward's life. Mysteriously, it fell to the ground soon after his death.

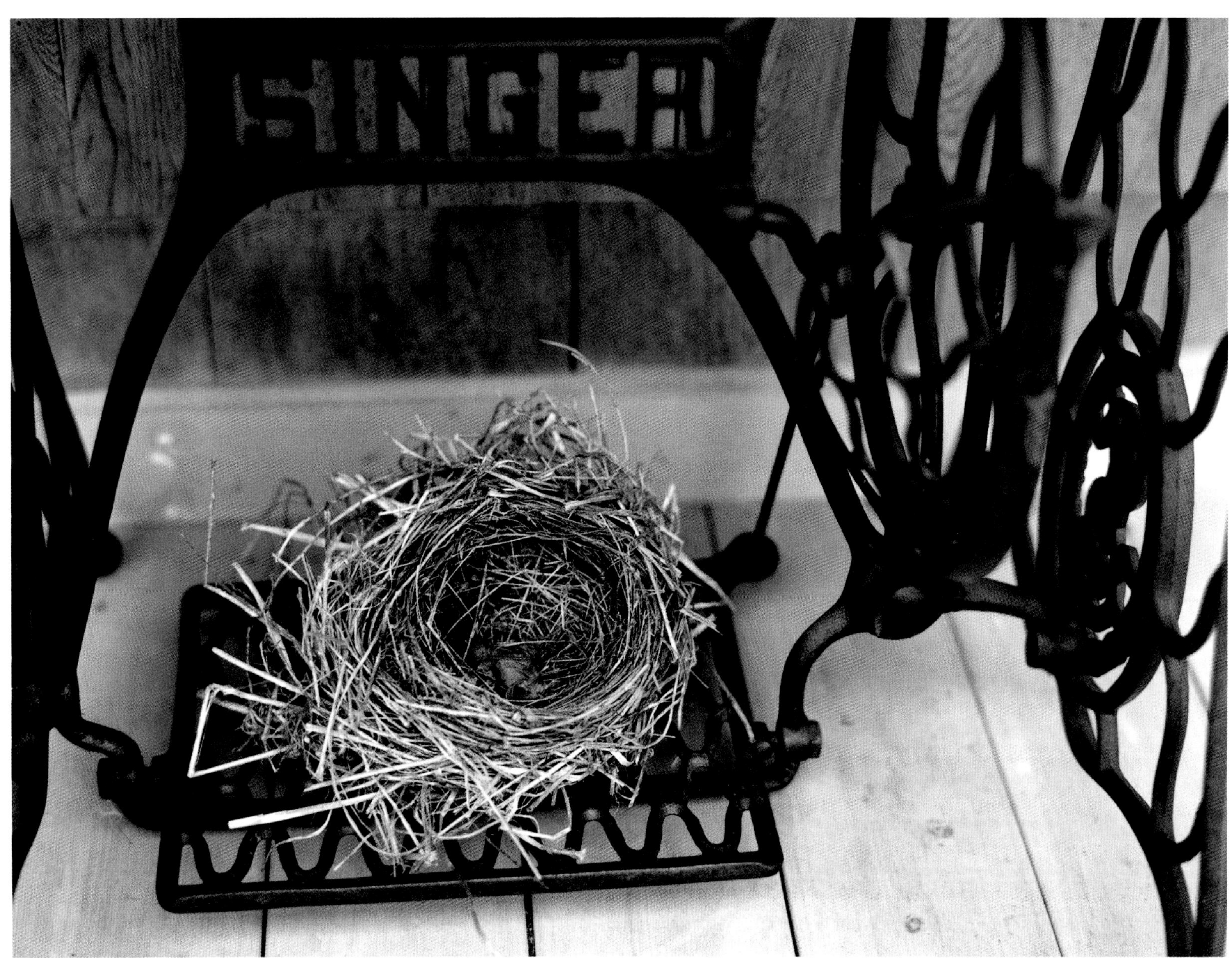
SINGER

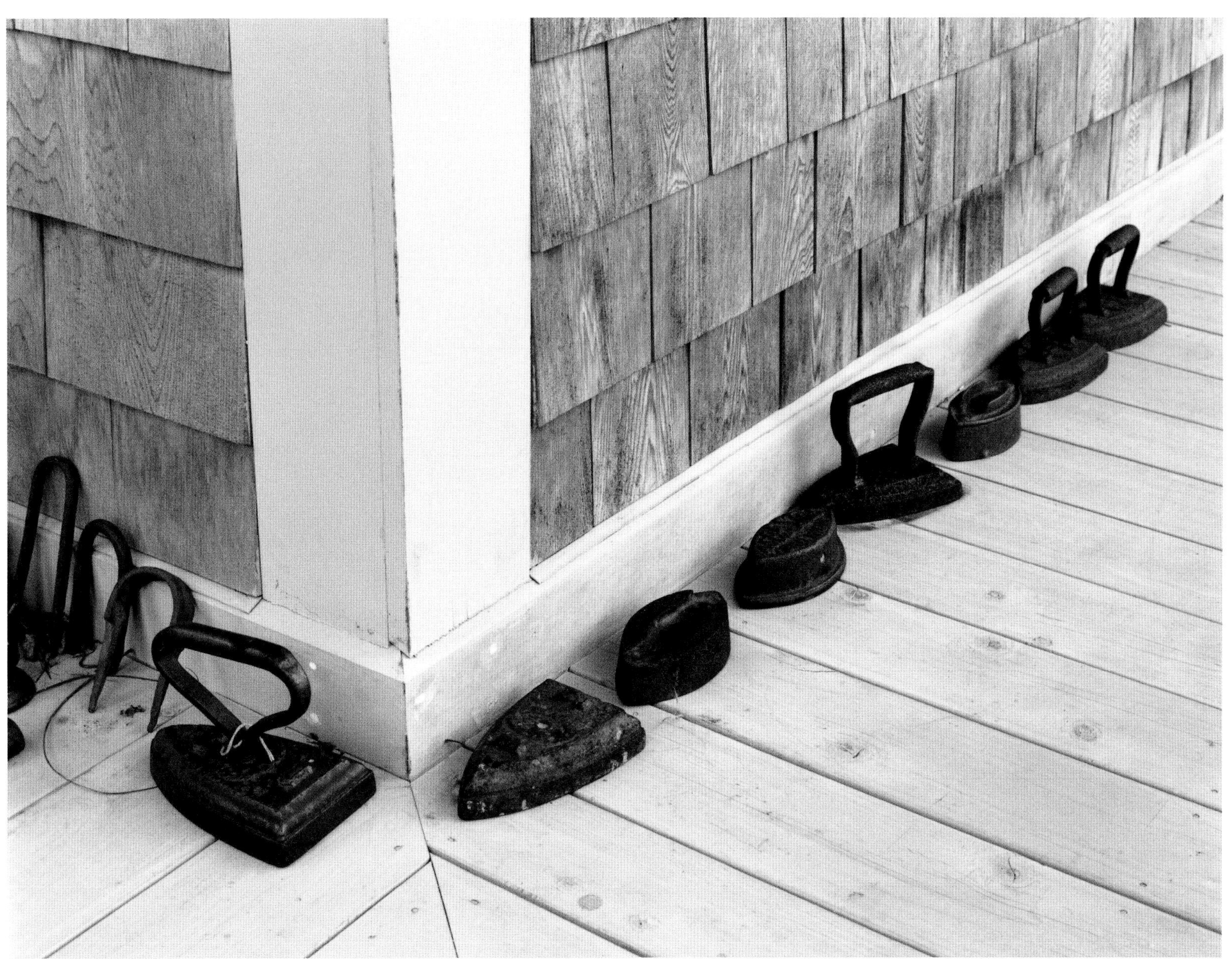

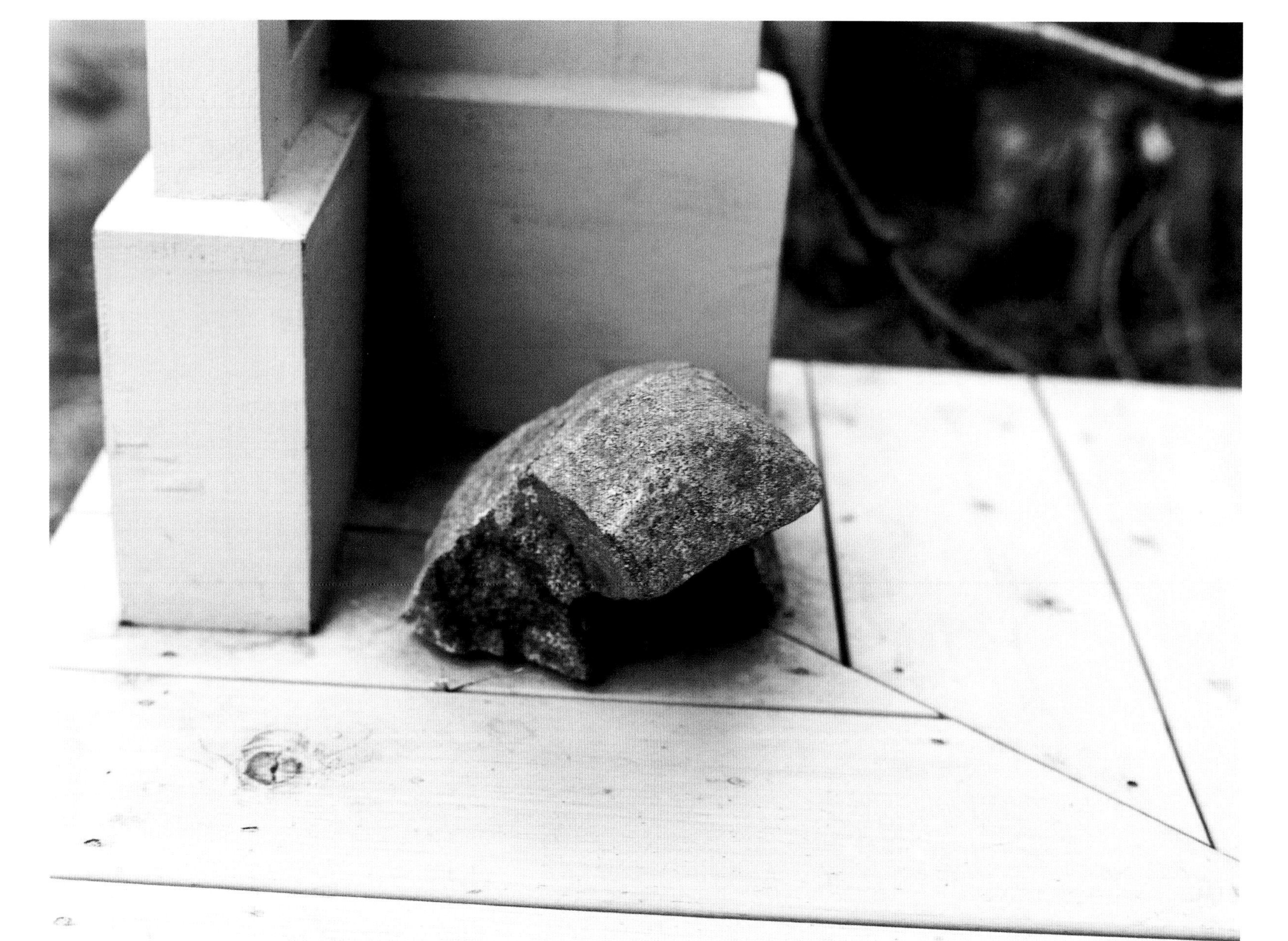

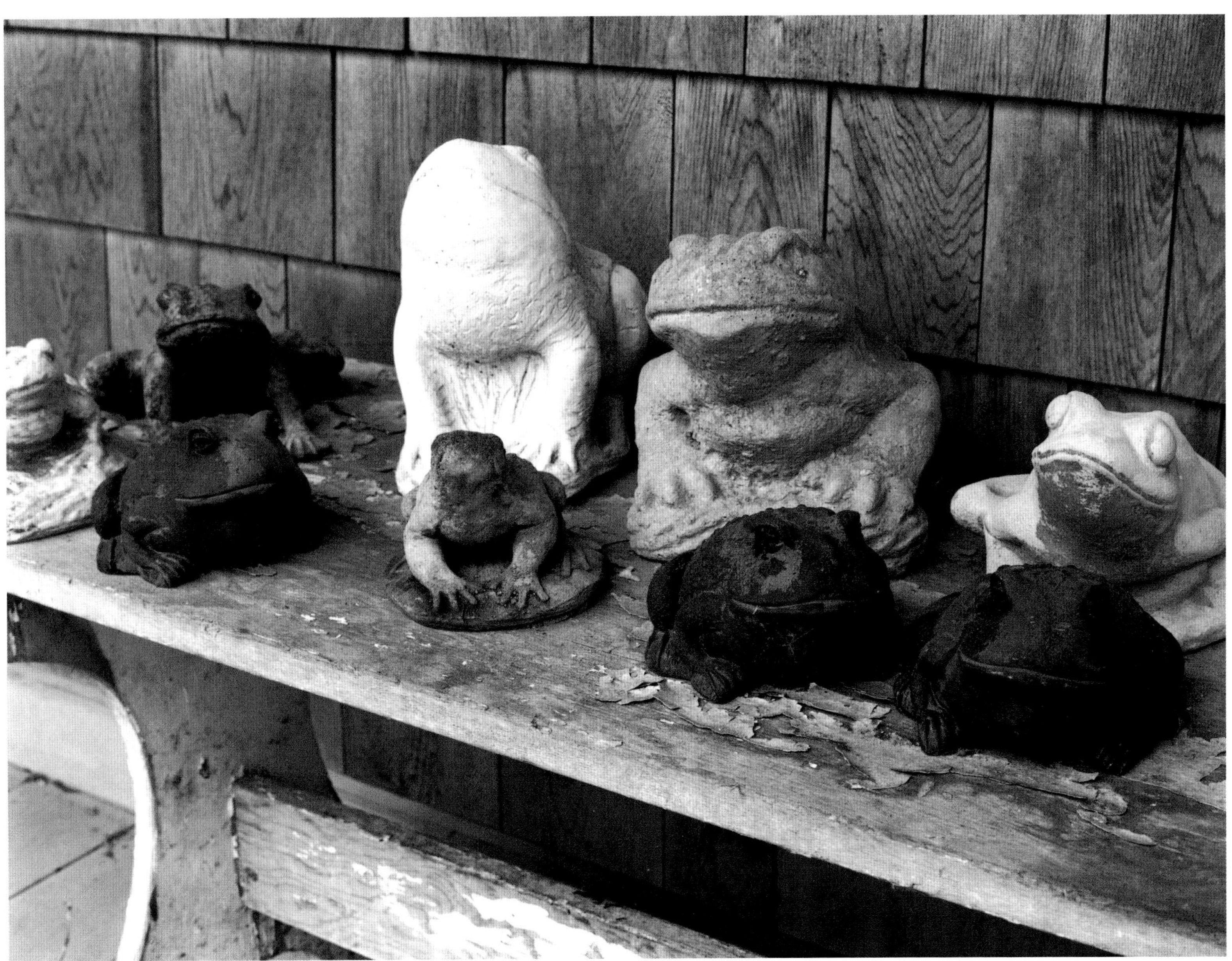

He drew out fifteen thousand pounds
  And bought a villa on the grounds.

The cousins kept eleven cats
  For whom they made becoming hats.

The trunk (along with other things)
  Held nineteen dozen curtain rings.

—Edward Gorey, from *Piermont Quartet Counting Book*

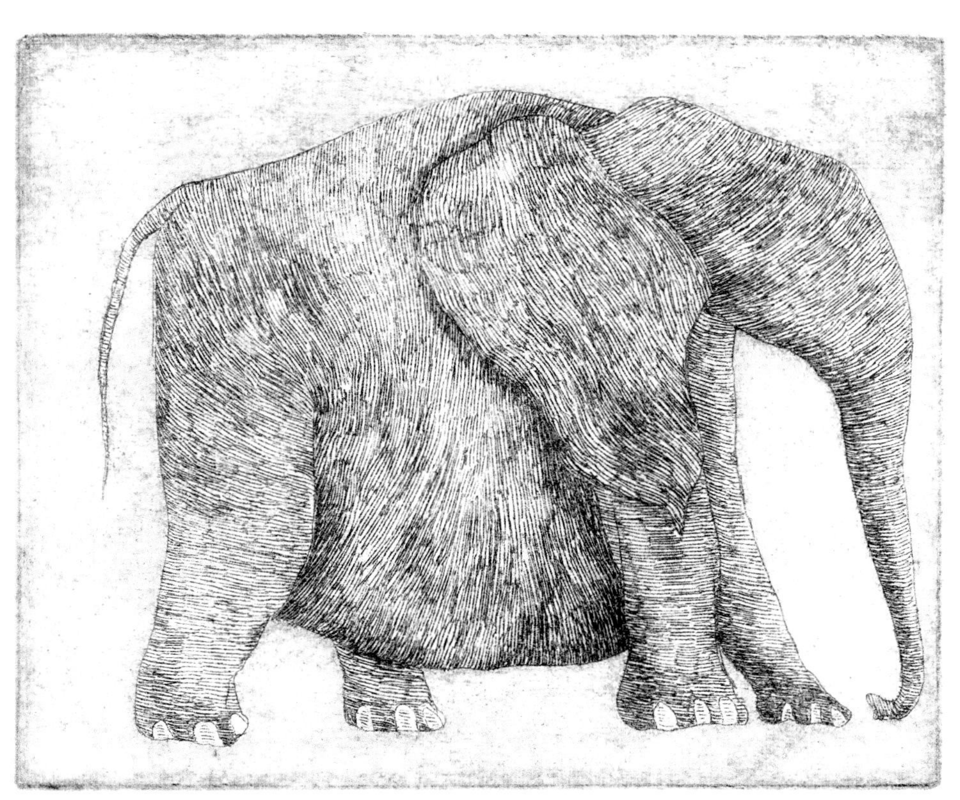

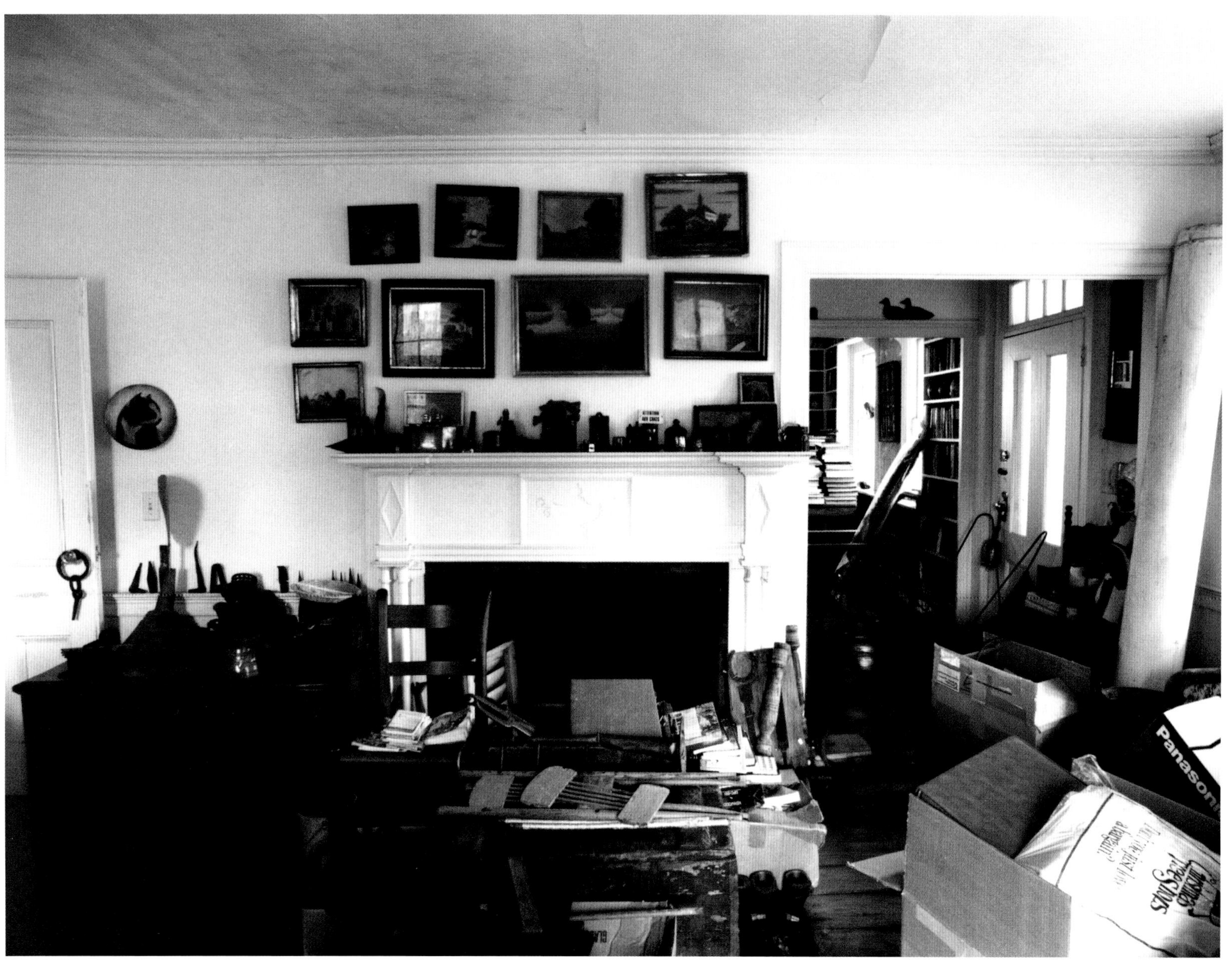
Panasoni

The Entrance Room

A visitor usually entered Edward's house through the door on the north side of the porch, which faced Route 6A. In this entrance room Edward displayed over the fireplace his collection of wonderful sand paintings, found at antique shops. He had been attracted to them "early in the game" and was proud of his judgment. Several oversized columns, also found in antique shops on the Cape, leaned against the corners of the room. Antiquing was an ongoing adventure for Edward. One of his favorite shops on the Cape was in Mashpee. Mel, Alex, and Edward would set out for "five miles off the map," so termed because the shop was five miles beyond the edge of their only map.

Edward's entrance room was always filled with boxes, lots of boxes. It functioned as a delivery and departure room for the entire house. There were cartons of Figbash mugs, remaining from the latest Gorey theater production on the Cape, and boxes of books ordered from Gotham Book Mart in New York City, awaiting a helping hand to move them to the library on the second floor. The large cardboard box that contained the television, installed years earlier, still remained. While Edward enjoyed receiving gifts, a large bag of Christmas presents from the prior Christmas sat in the corner beside the legendary "elephant toilet" end table. One of Edward's handmade stuffed elephants held center stage on the fireplace mantle.

Edward's collections were eclectic, ranging from rare seventeenth-century pieces to objects found on the side of the road. When Edward first discovered the house he decided that he did not want closets. He preferred to keep things in old blanket chests. An entrance room chest (under a collection of old metal toy trains) contained over three hundred pounds of rusting metal objects, including machine parts, stakes for railroad ties, and old tools. Edward had a fondness for the texture of decay.

Panasonic

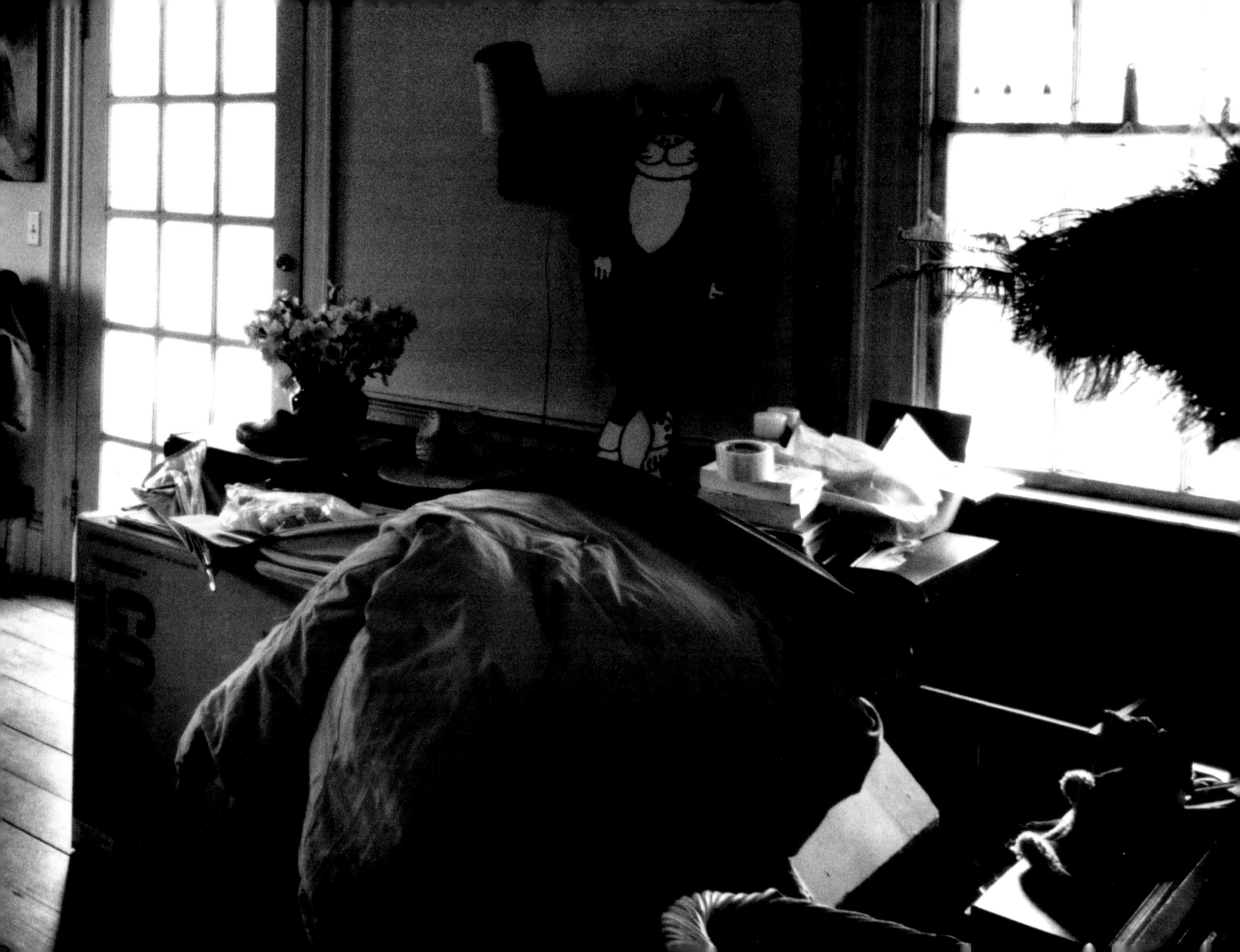

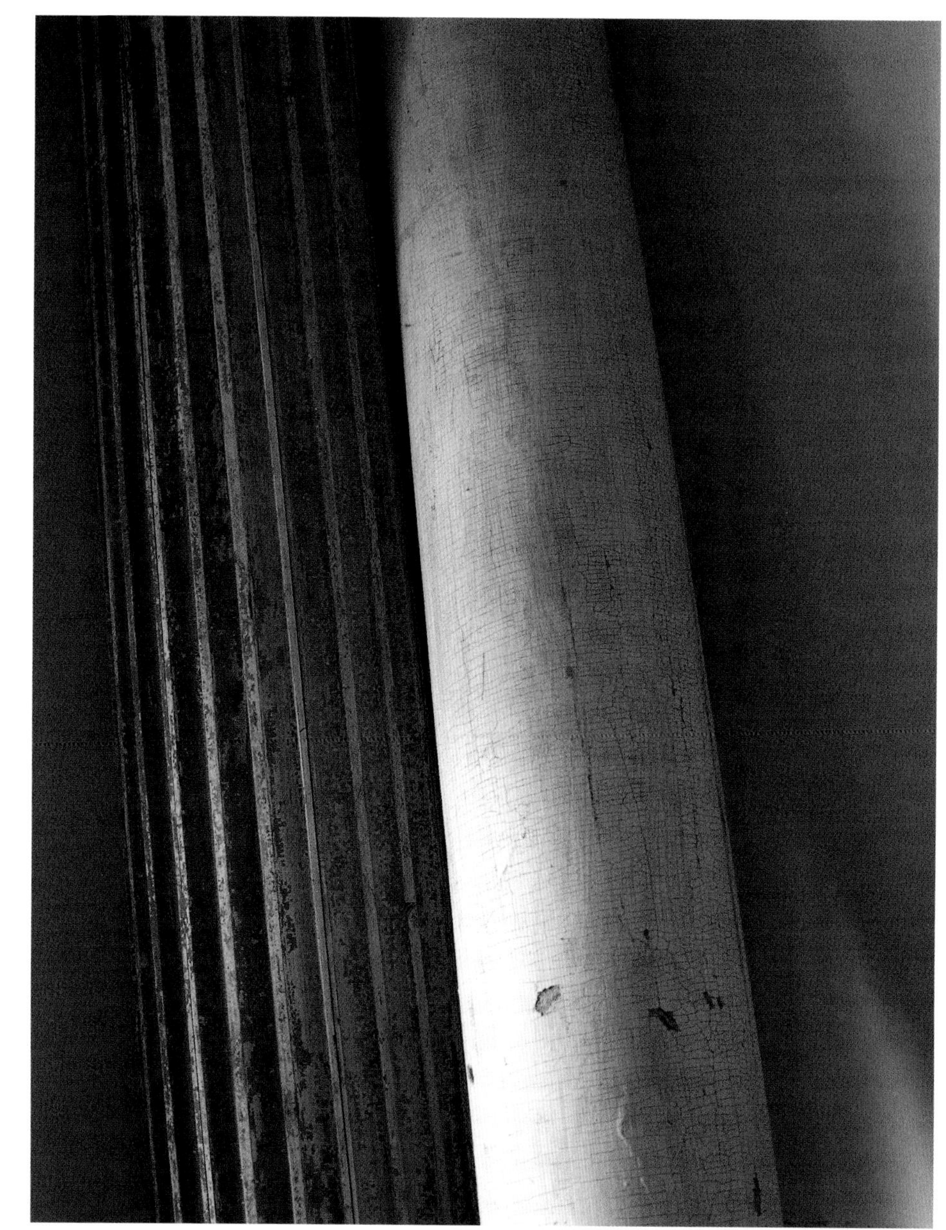

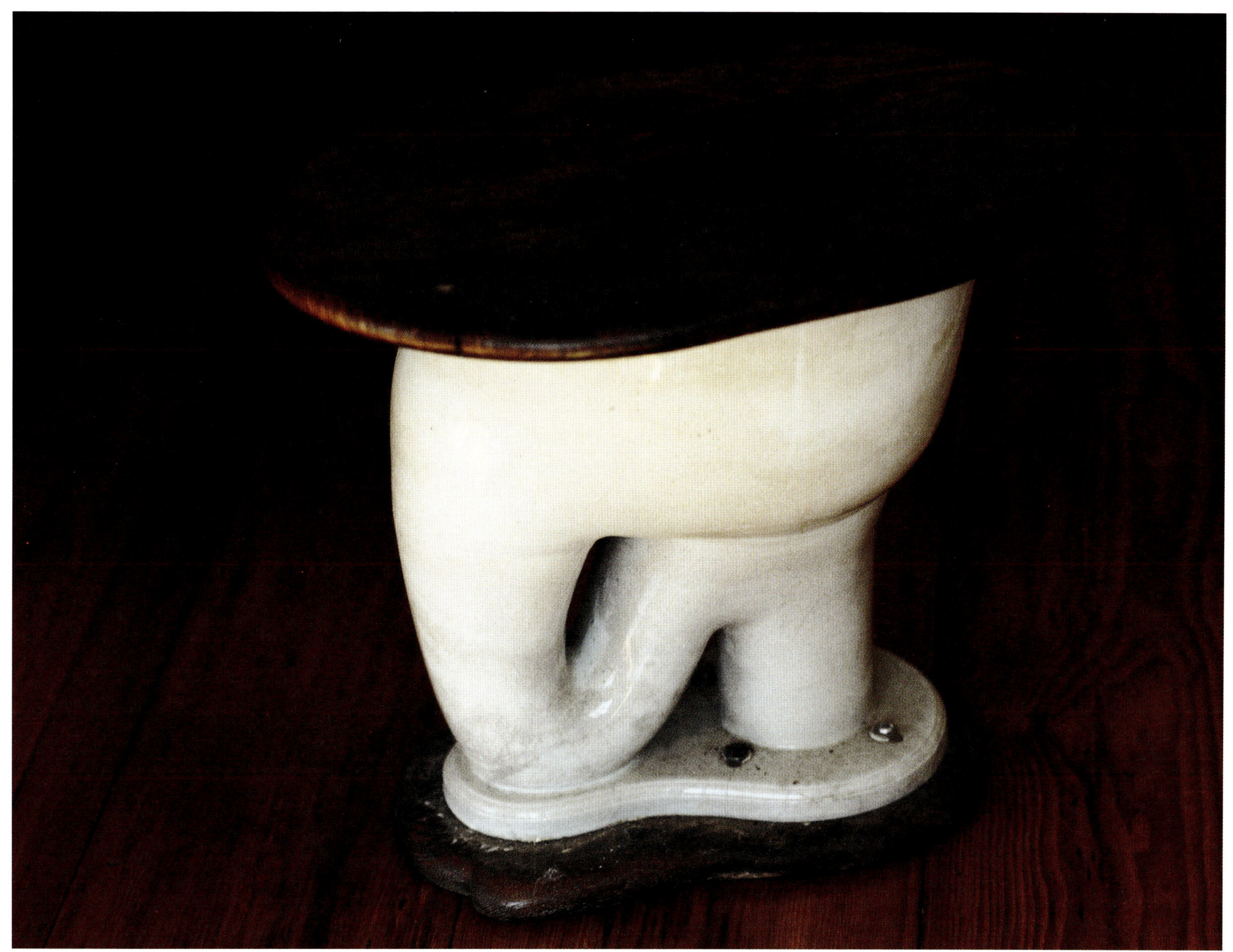

The furniture within this room
  Does nothing to dispel its gloom.

Some awful thing has happened here,
  Though what is not entirely clear.

And this is how a person's head
  Will look long after he is dead.

—Edward Gorey, from *Piermont Quartet Picture Book*

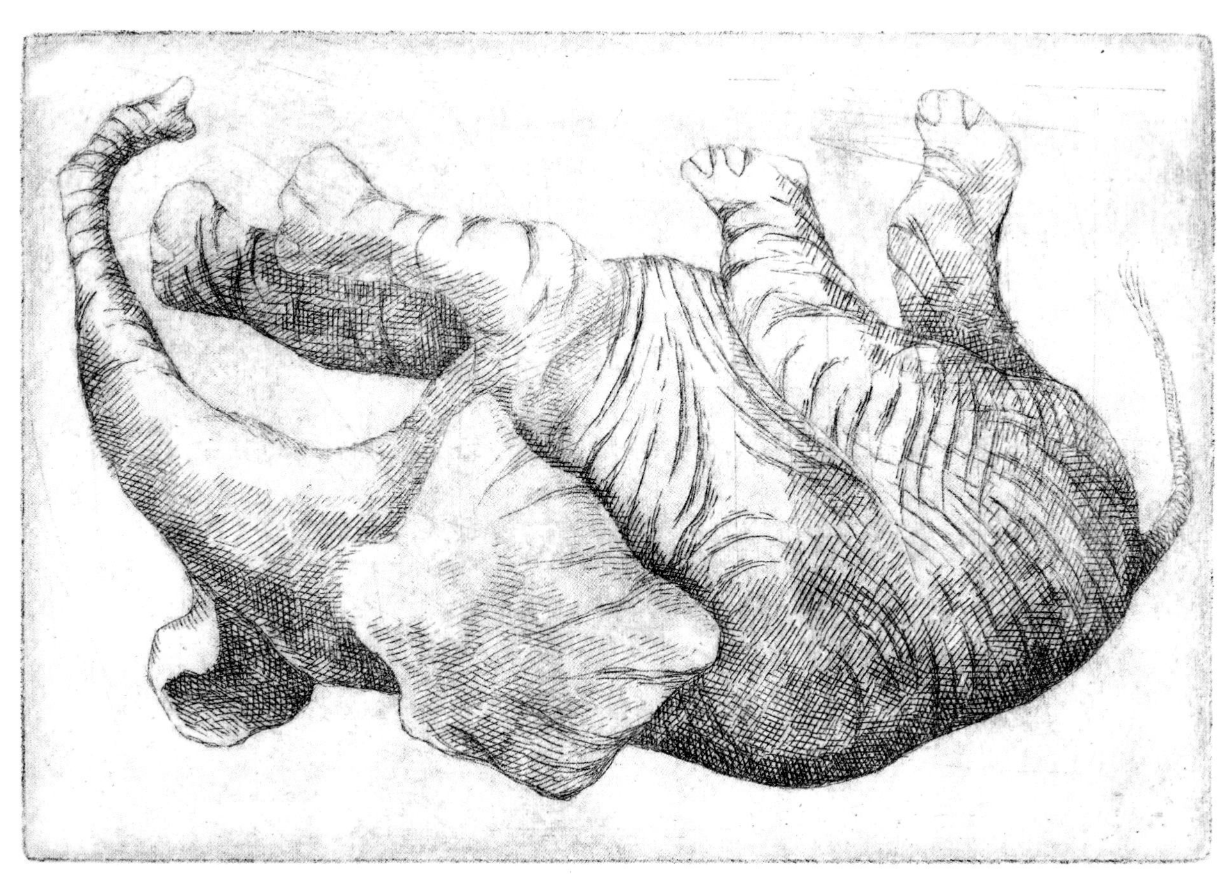

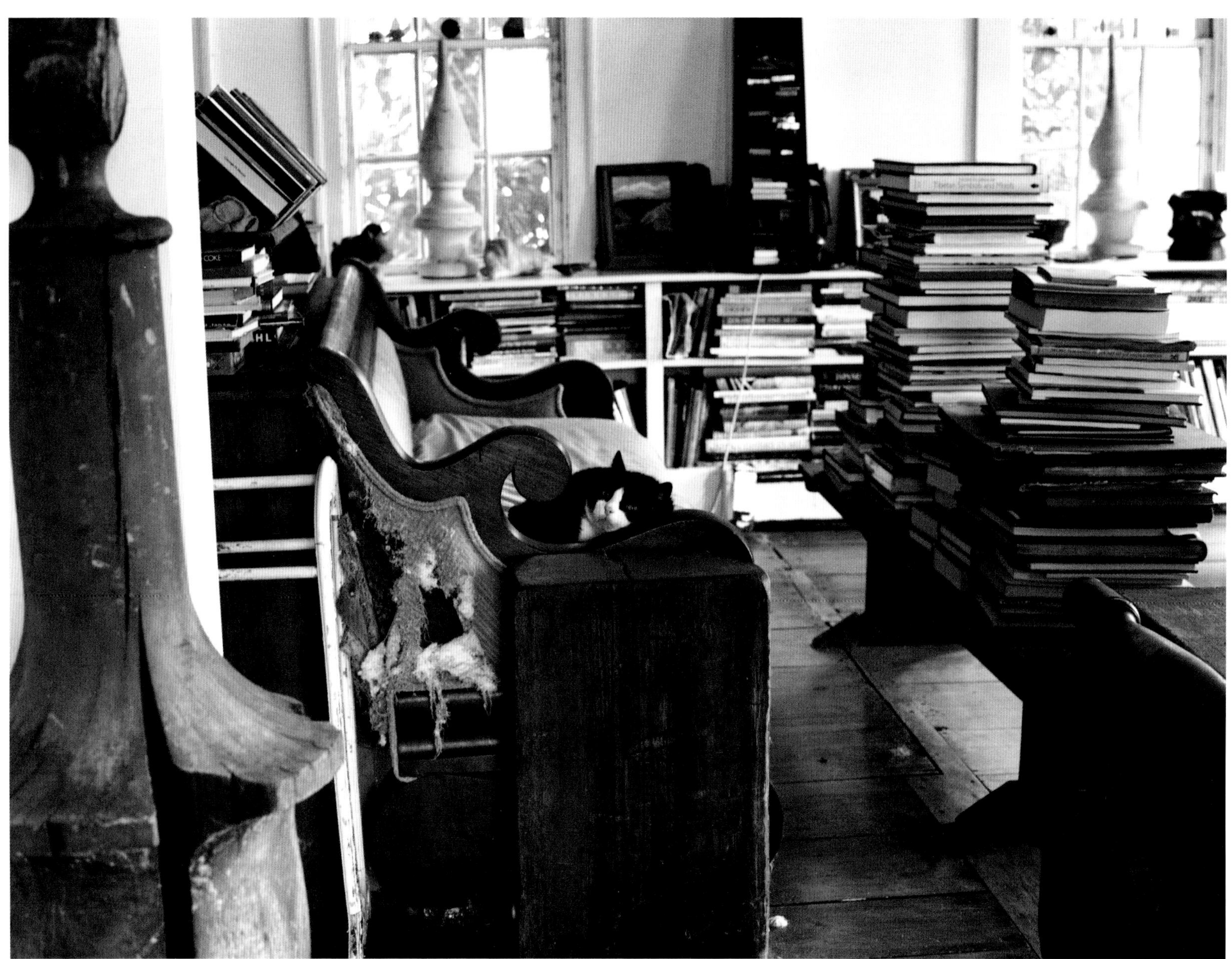

The Living Room

Edward appreciated objects that indicated some degree of prior use—things that had had a life. During the early interior renovations of the house, he had the wallpaper removed in this room, revealing a subtle, early painted plasterwork. It had a faded pink coloration with a faint stencil design. Edward never painted or replastered those walls. The sofa in the living room was inherited from his family. A few of Edward's cats (Weadon, Jane, and George) decided to make it theirs and set about destroying the upholstery. In fact, the cats had complete run of the house. And yes, when you entered the house, you knew the cats were there.

Edward collected finials of all sizes, from two inches to five feet in height. He also liked old wooden potato mashers. When he found twenty painted eggs in a shop and saw their "potential," he bought all twenty. Although he collected fine art (works by Delacroix, Vuillard, Bonnard, Balthus, Manet, and Burchfield were among his possessions), he also collected "kitsch" paintings. The fact that someone had spent the time painting and framing them intrigued him. He truly enjoyed these works. Edward's appreciation of high and low art crossed all genres. Although he loved most early classical music, he also genuinely enjoyed country music (Lyle Lovett was a favorite during the last years of Edward's life).

During a visit to a local antique shop, Edward discovered that an artist had taken old paned window frames and replaced each pane of glass with a mirror. He was quite taken with the idea and bought several of them, placing them in various rooms throughout the house. The effect of seeing several slightly different views of the same scene pleased him.

On the far south side of the room was a set of three large windows and an elegantly paned fanlight window. These windows provided year-round sun and a beautiful view of open greenery. It was a favorite spot for Edward. He sat at the window table, working on one of his many manual typewriters, purchased at various yard sales over the years. However, these windows had their problems. A vine of poison ivy once stubbornly grew through the windows' frame edge and remained undisturbed until the house was finally reshingled. The fanlight window had a persistent leak, and as a result, everything stored in the cabinet below was destroyed. Edward was very fond of colored glass. His accumulation ranged from rare antique cut pieces to colored fragments found along the shore. He placed them on the window ledges in every room of the house. This of course posed a problem when opening windows.

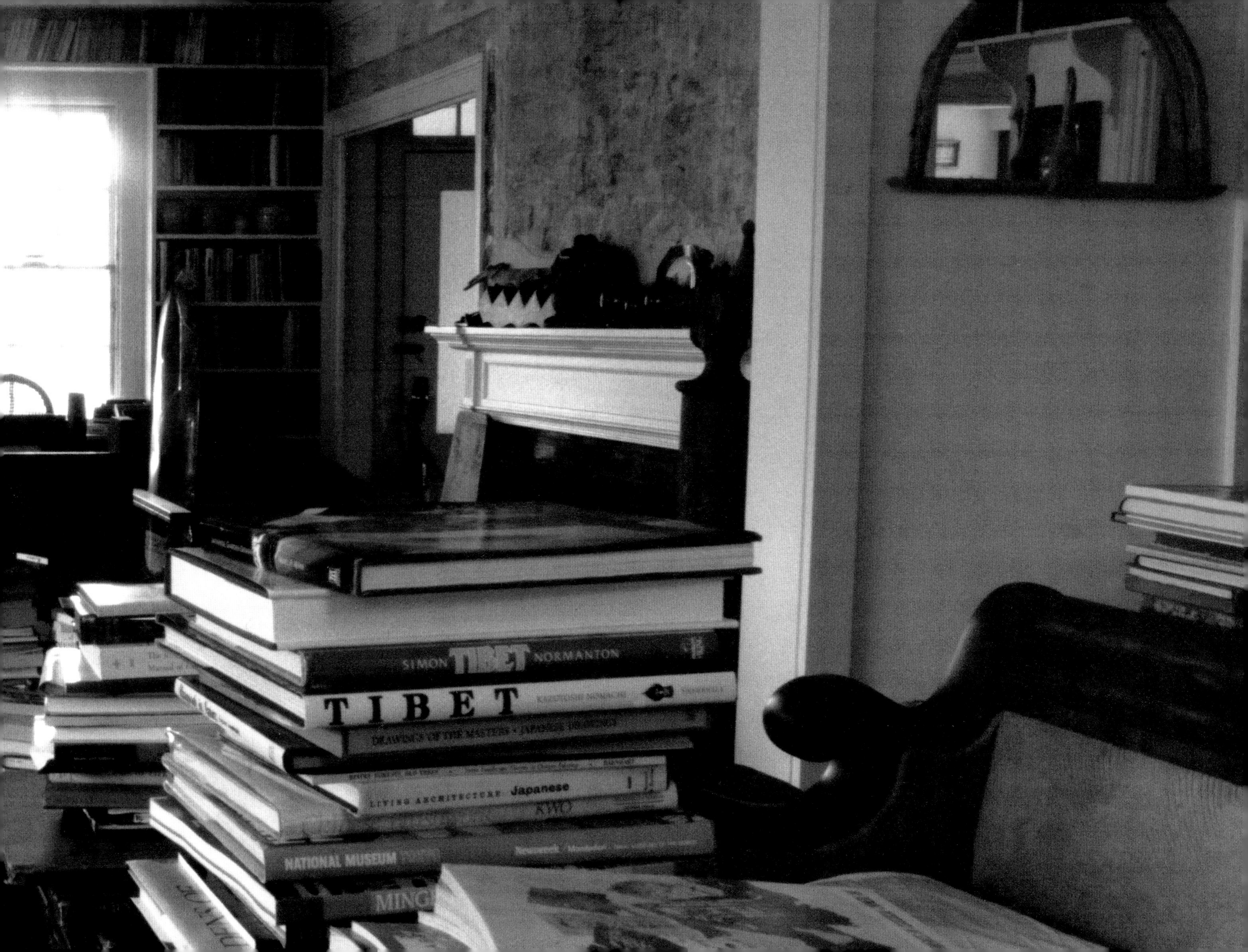
SIMON TIBET NORMANTON
TIBET
LIVING ARCHITECTURE Japanese
NATIONAL MUSEUM

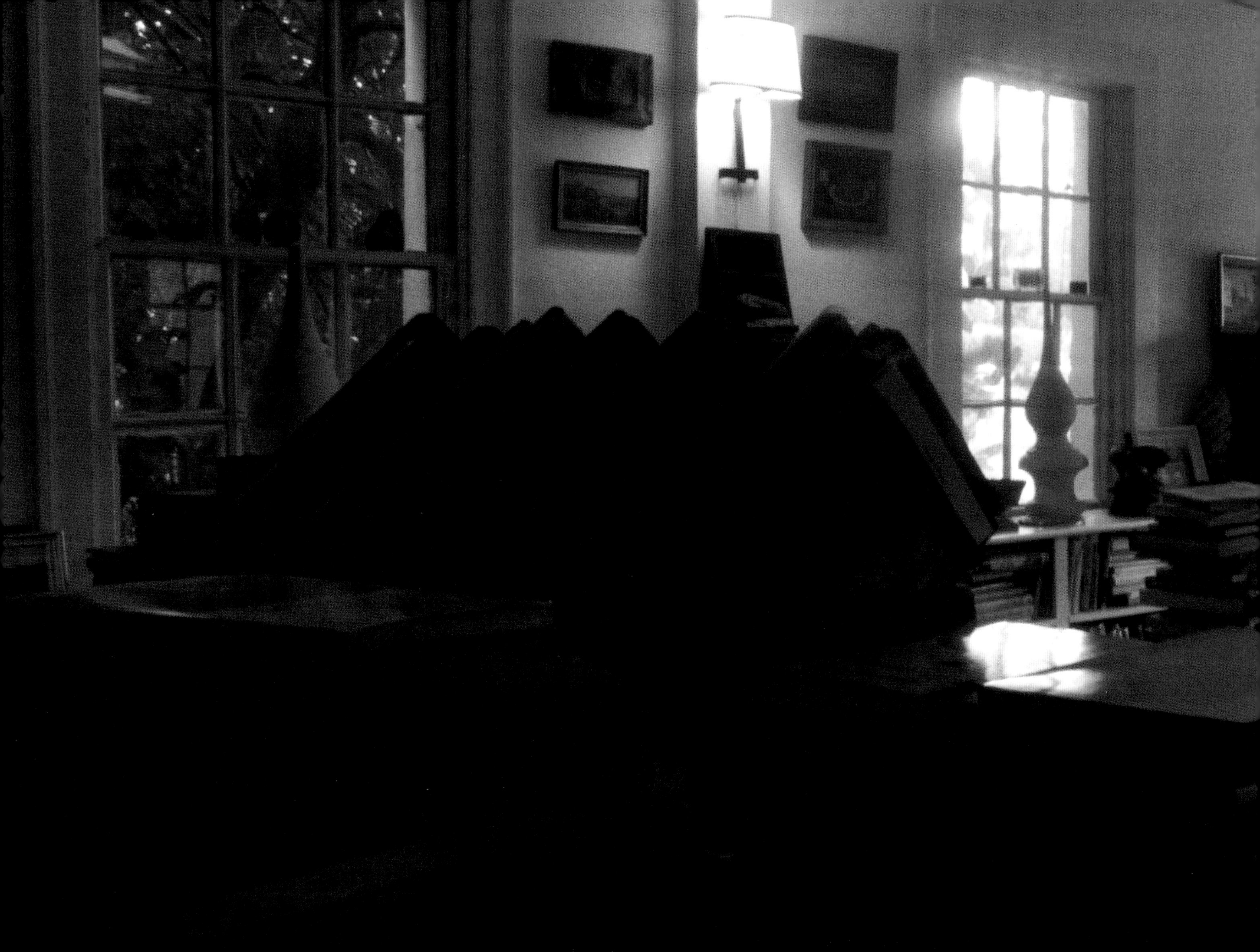

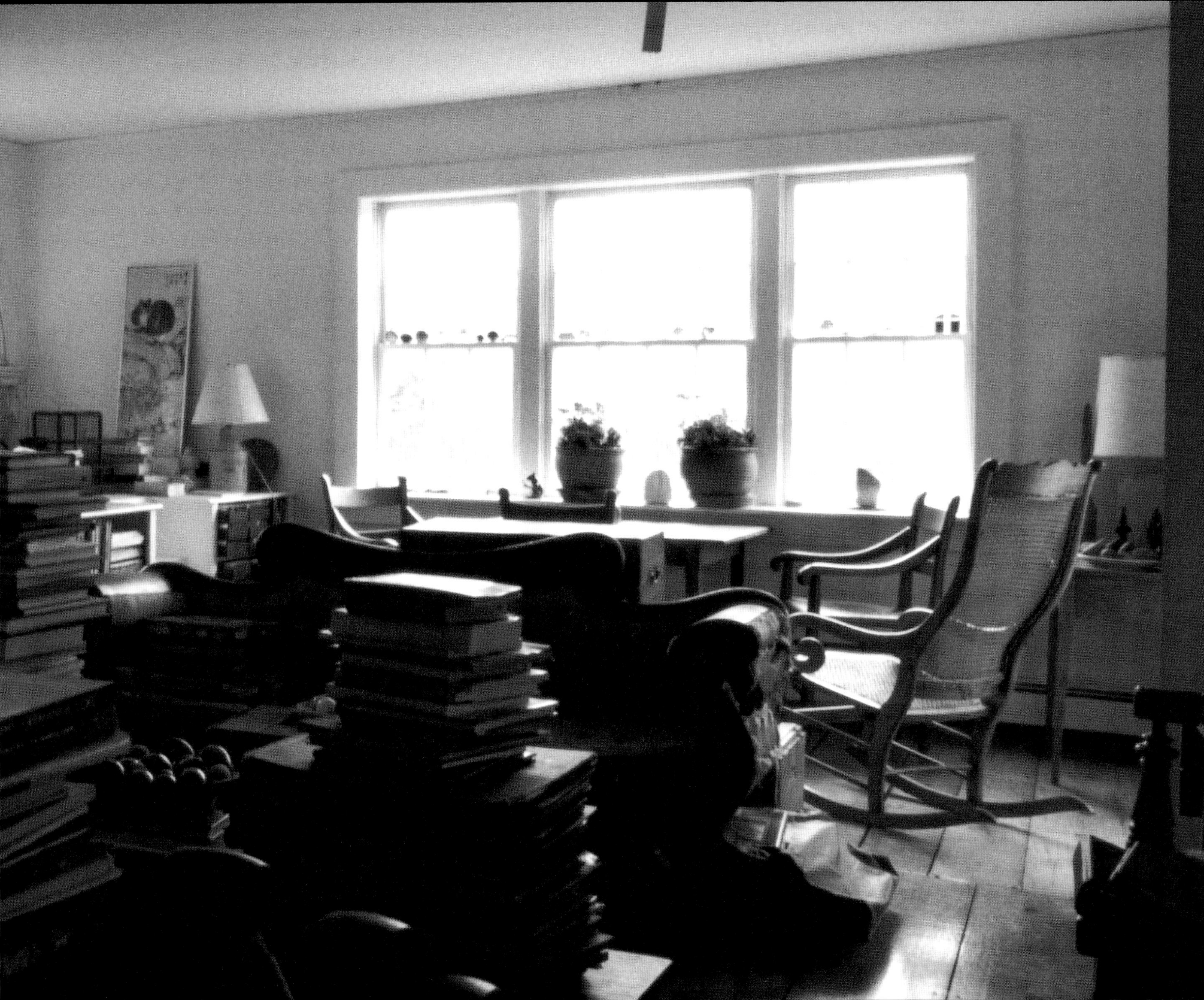

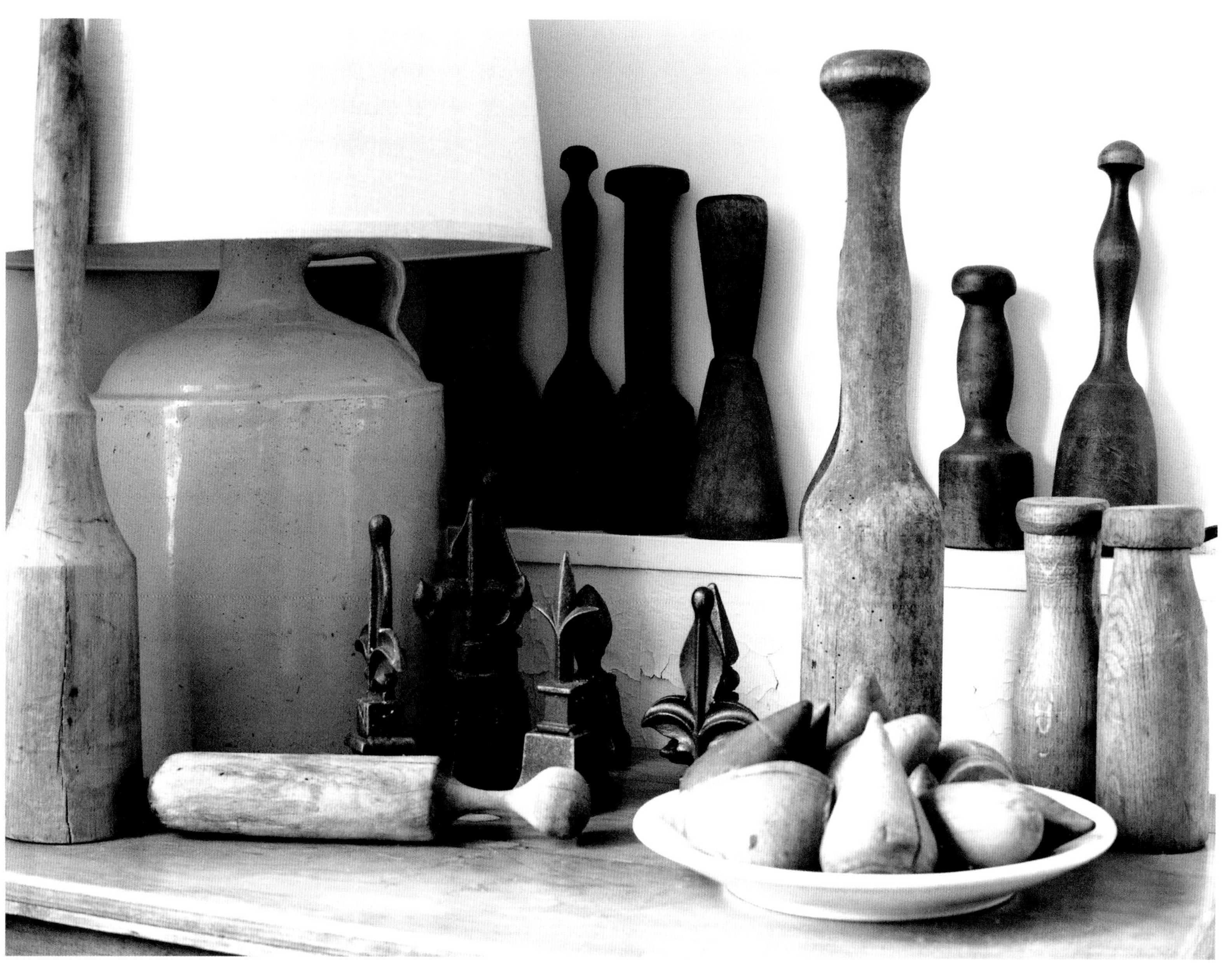

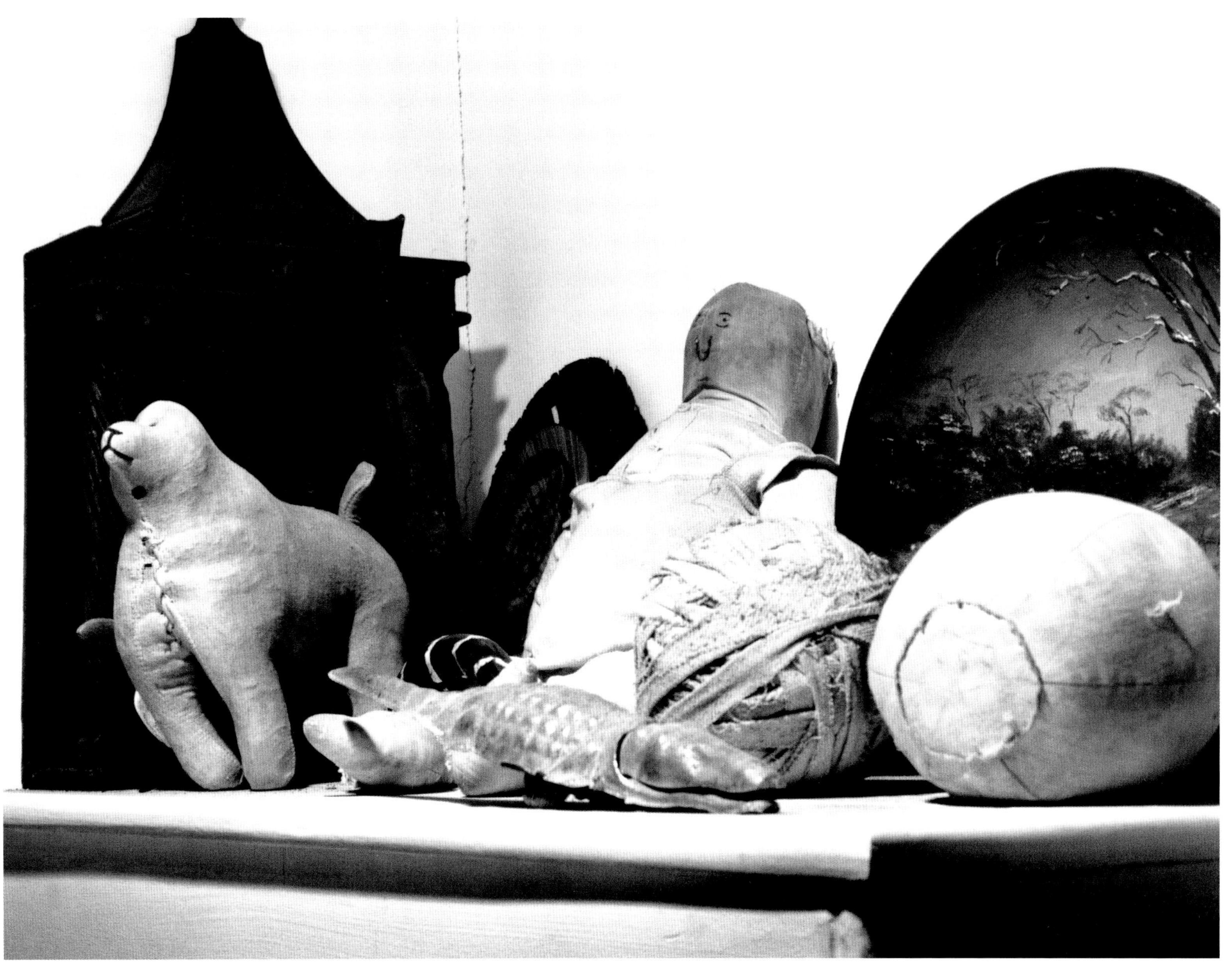

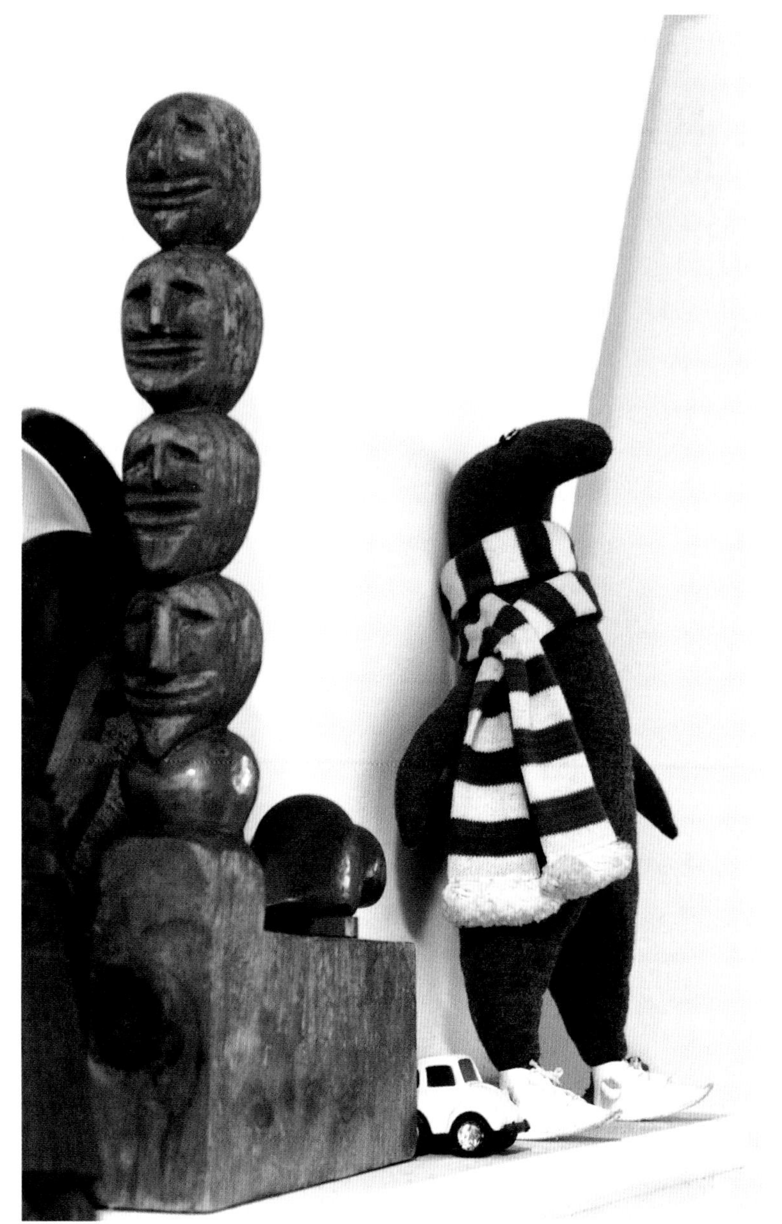

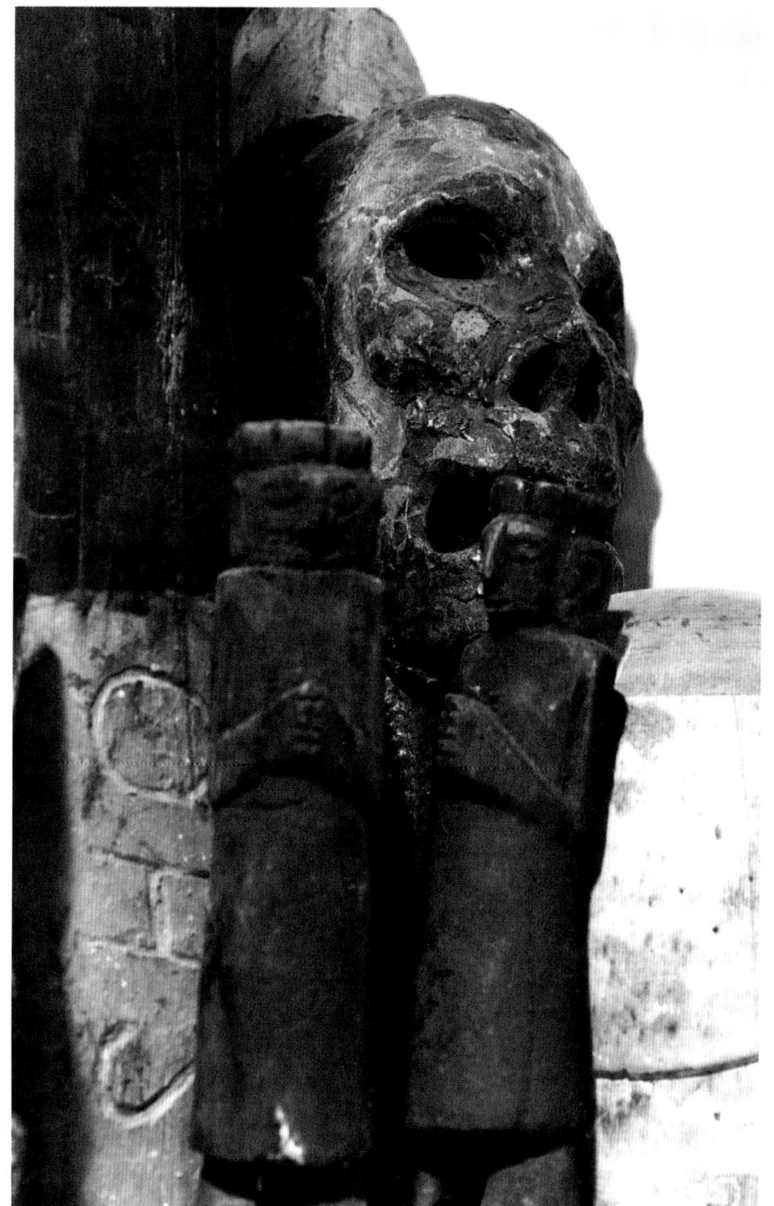

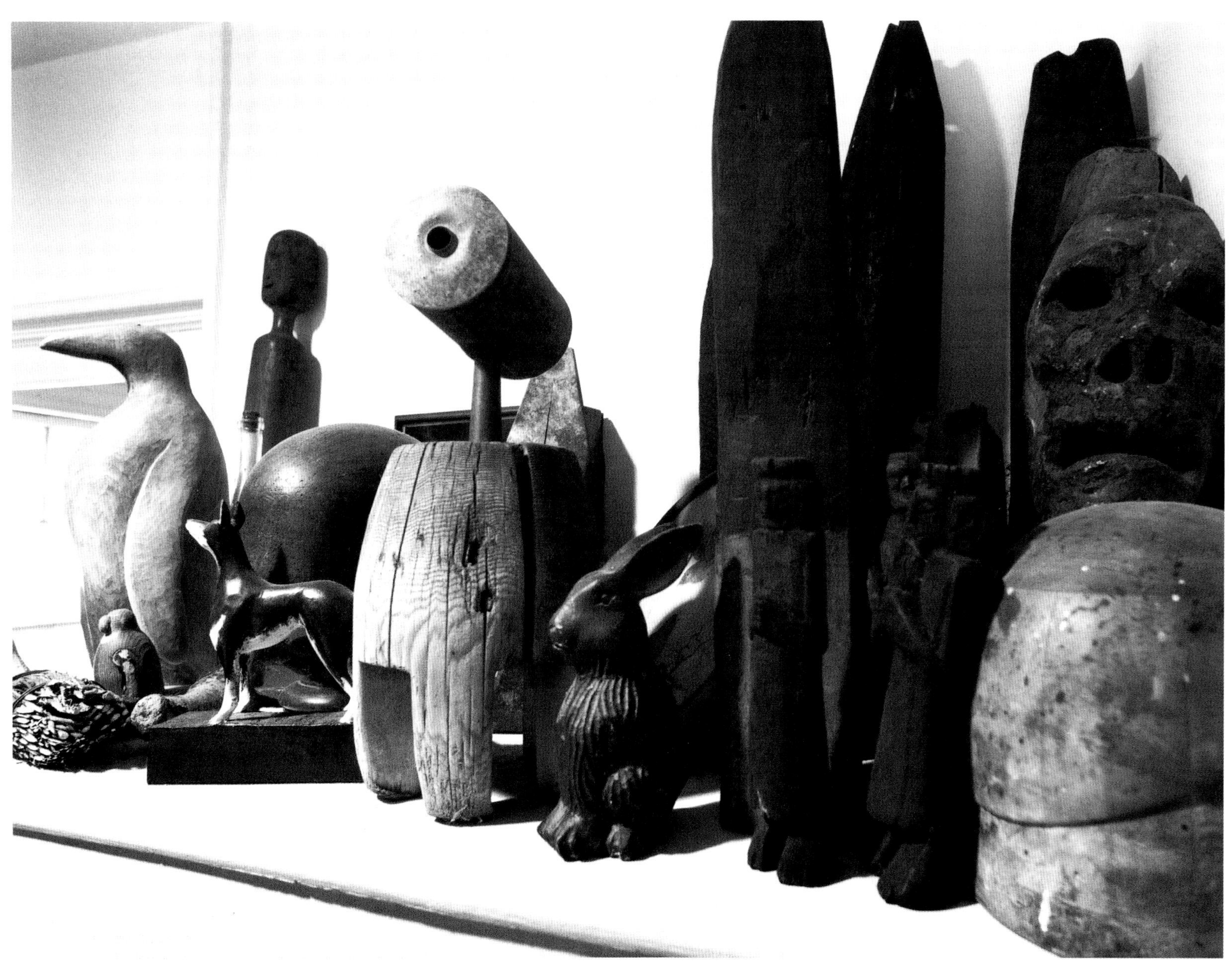

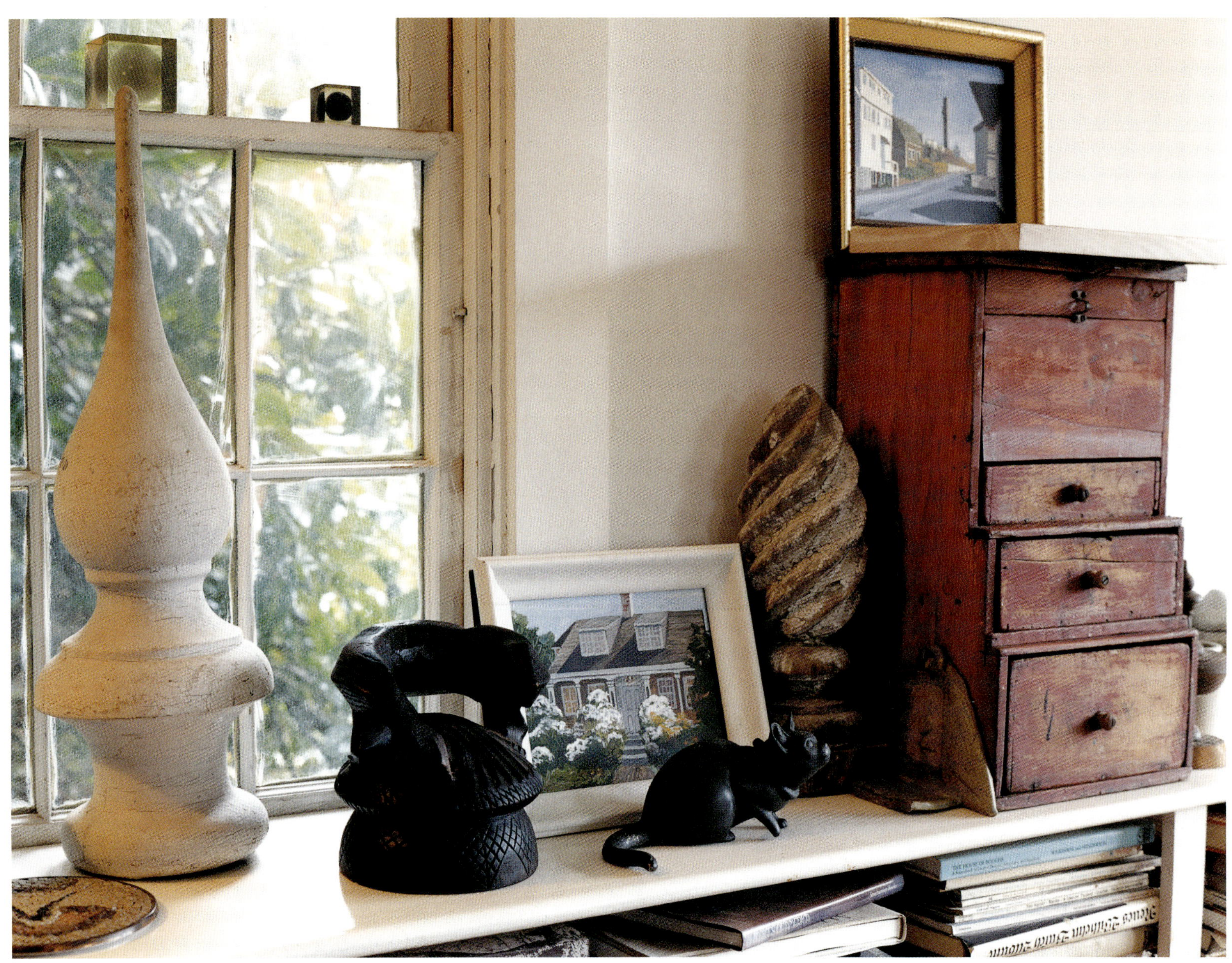

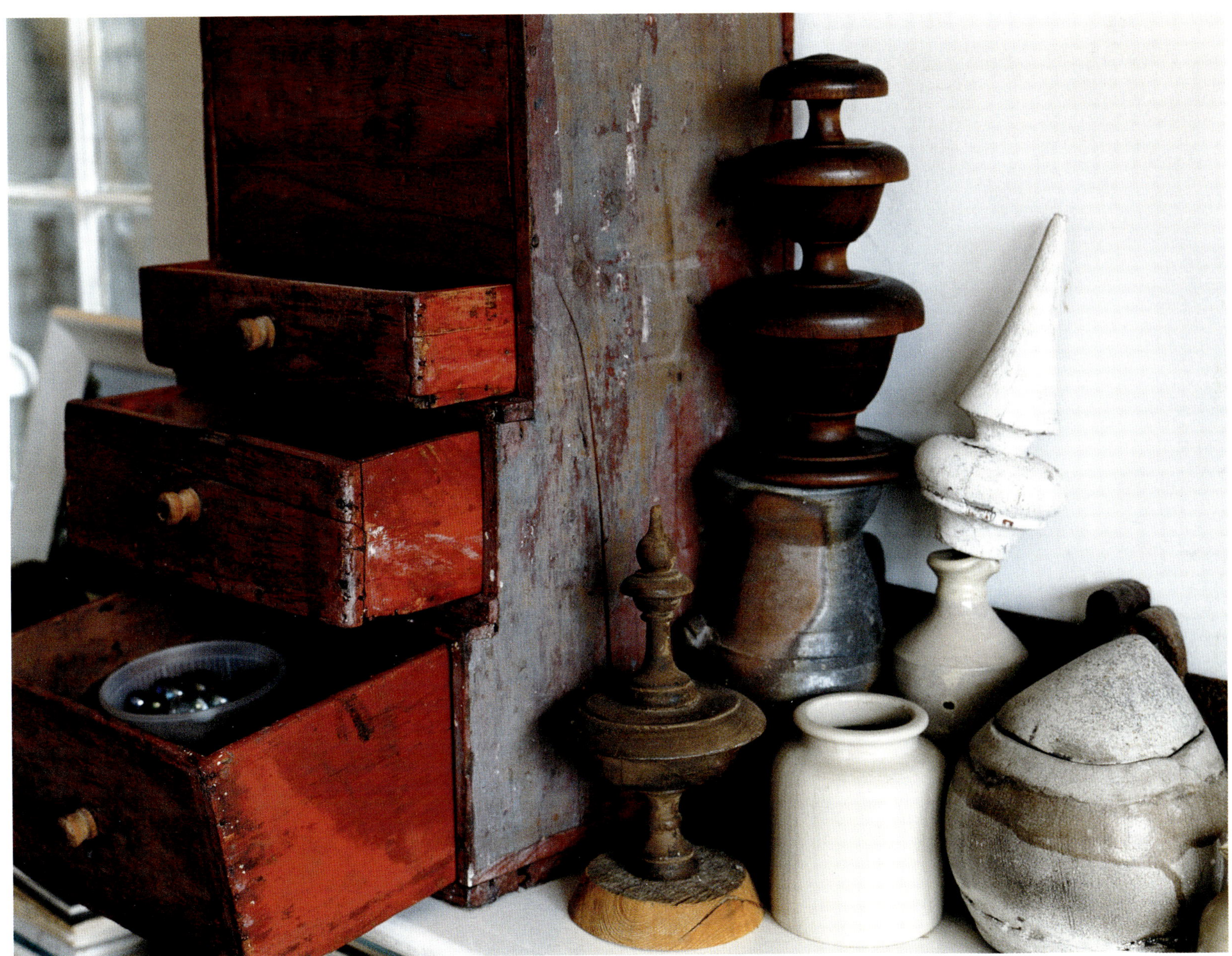

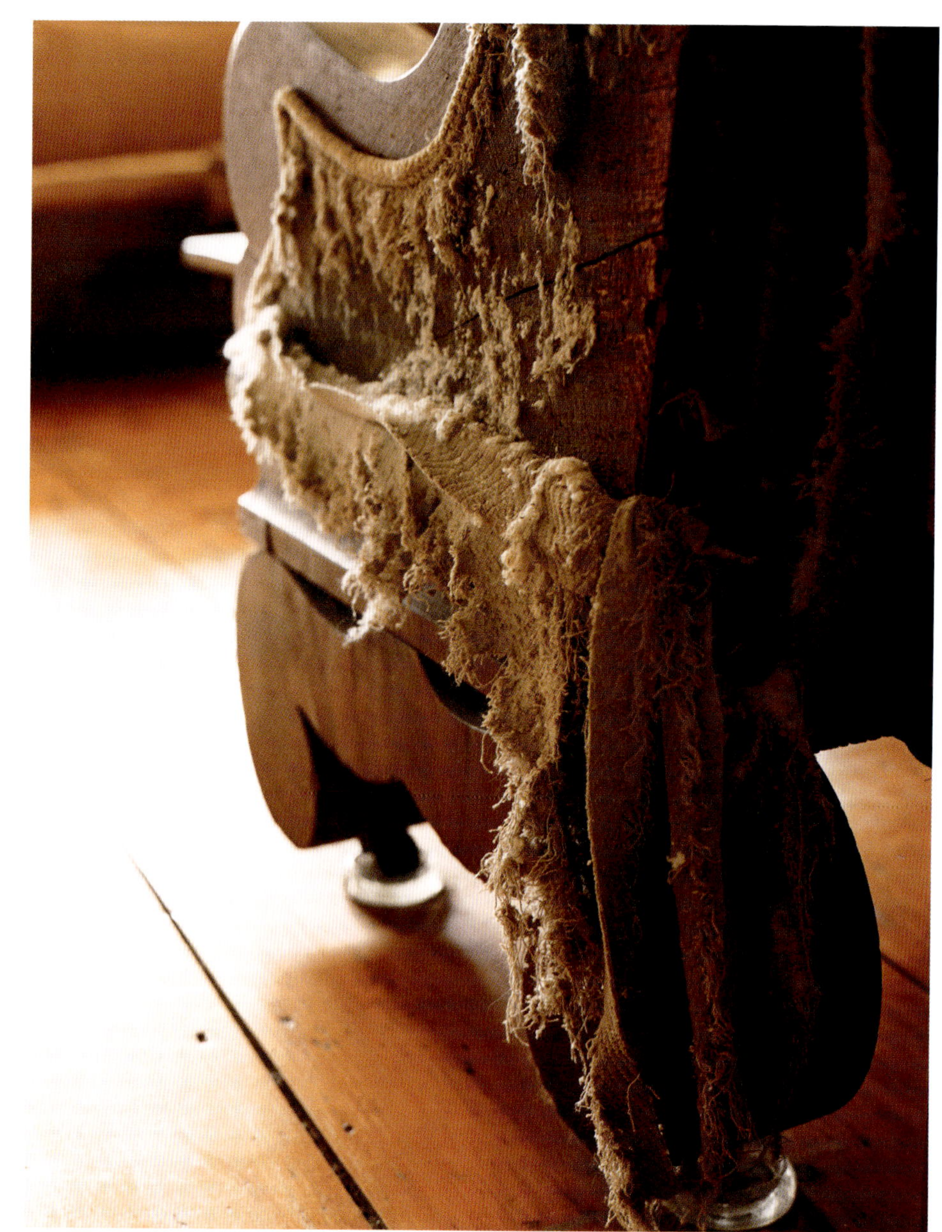

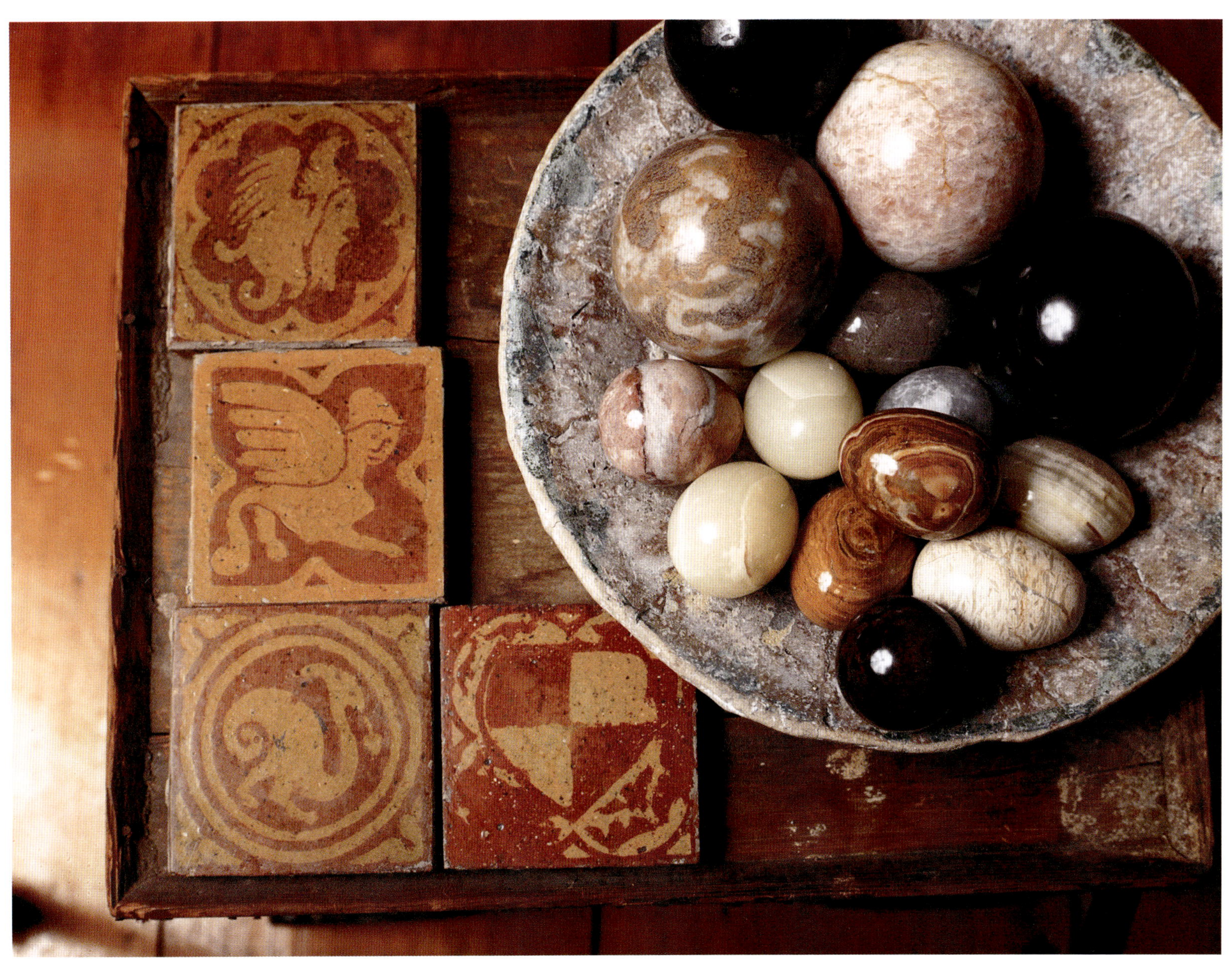

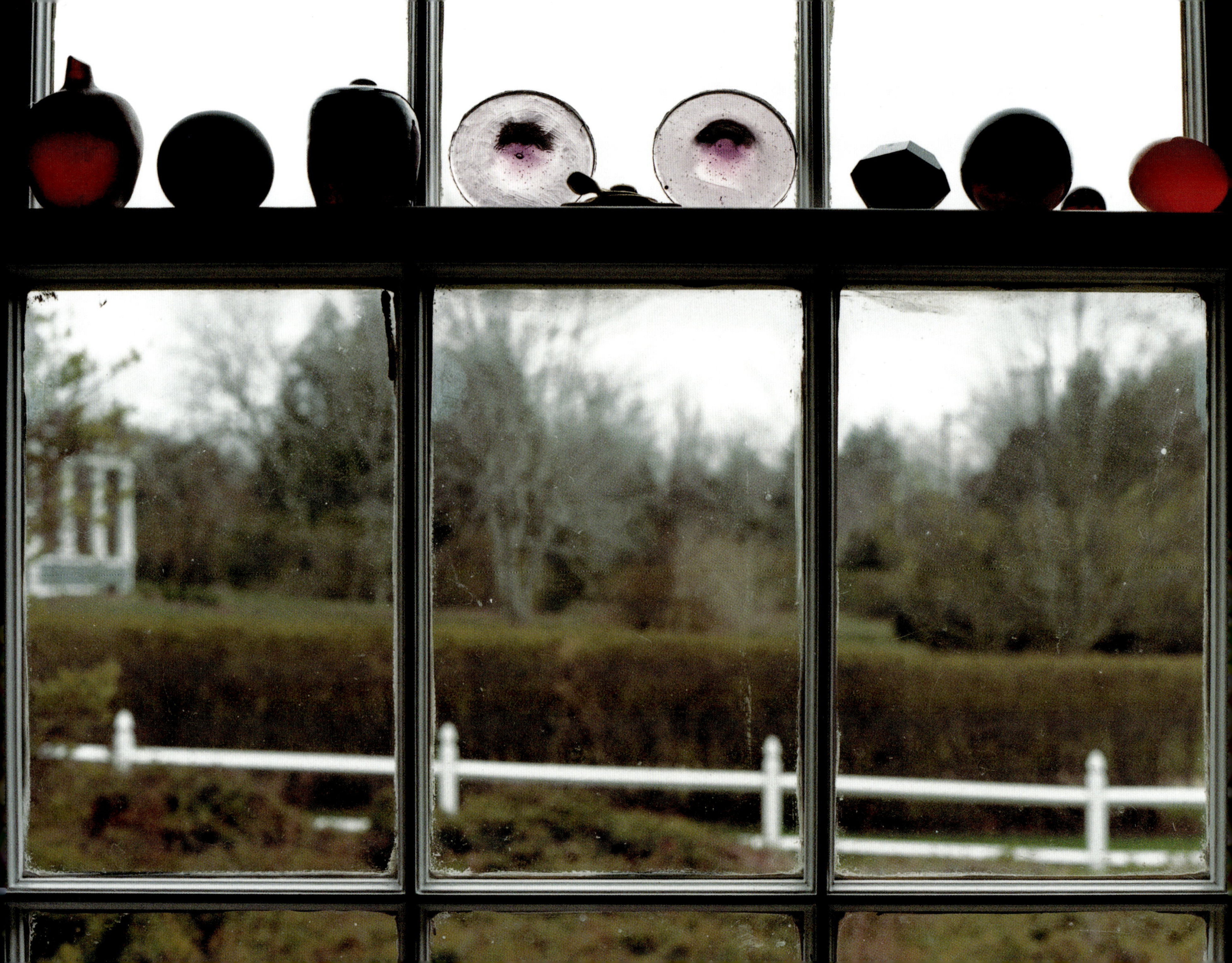

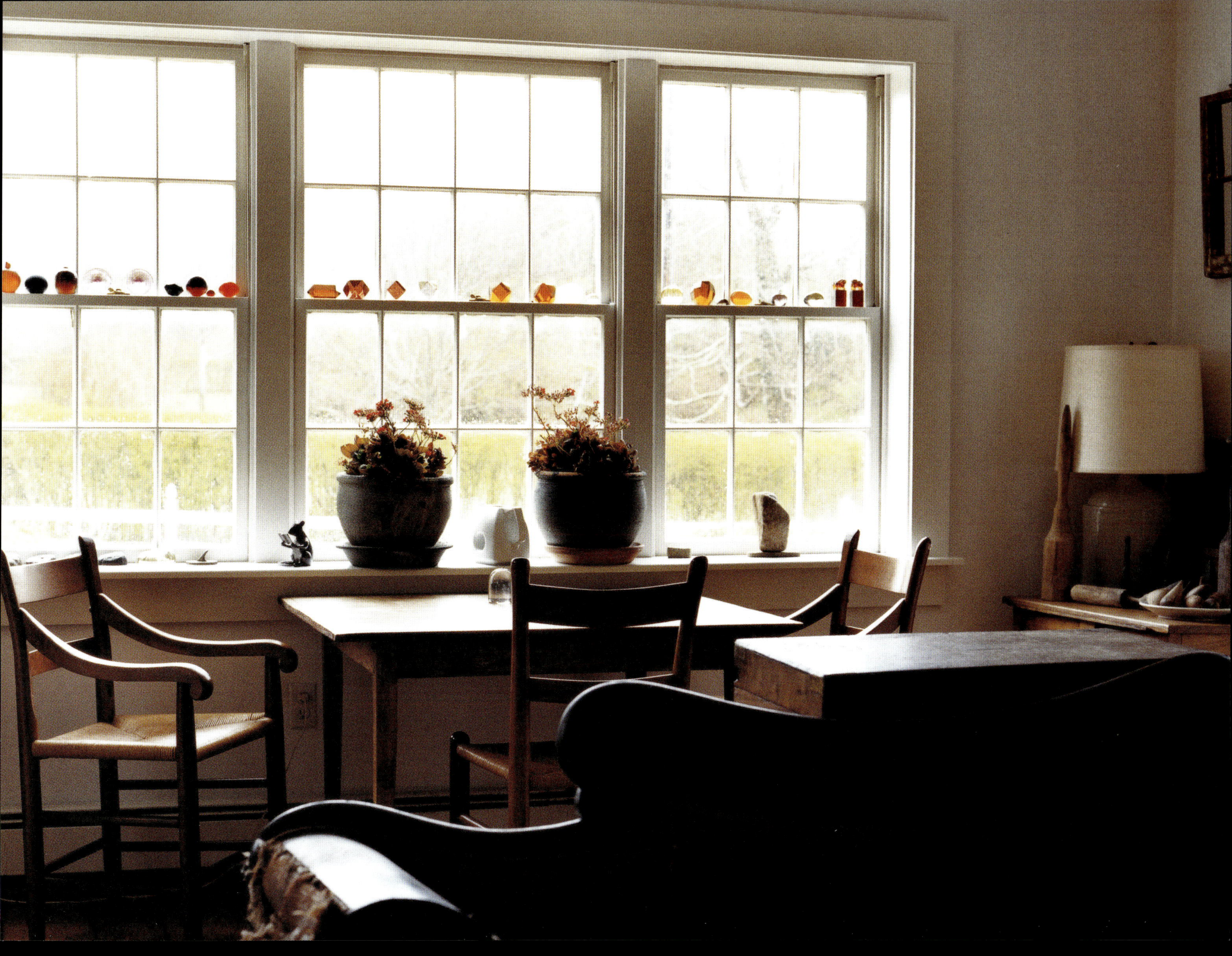

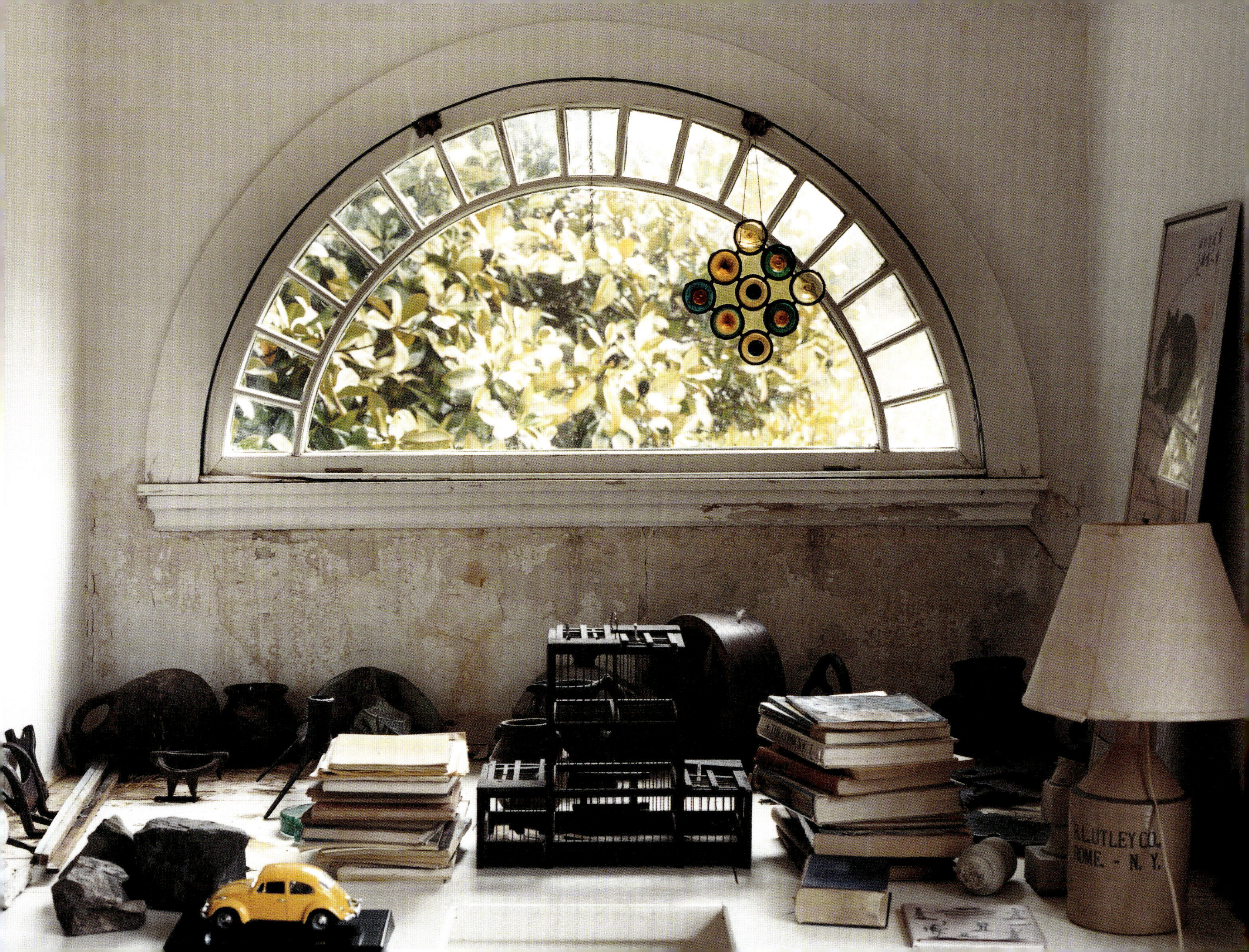
THE COMICS
R.L.UTLEY CO.
ROME. - N. Y.

In the ensuing weeks white sauce appeared at least once,
and often two or three times, at every meal, even breakfast.

The last of the sauce covered some ill-mashed turnips.

Just after the meal concluded Henry suddenly died.

—Edward Gorey, from *The Water Flowers*

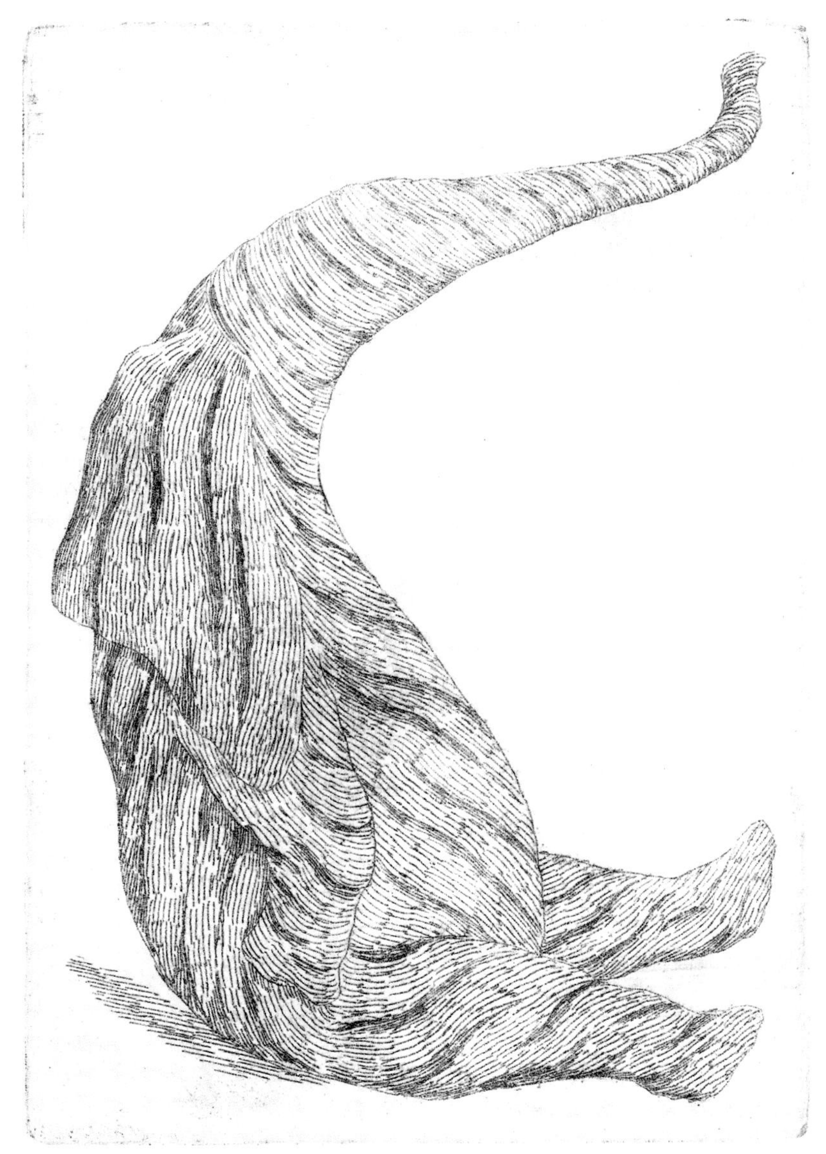

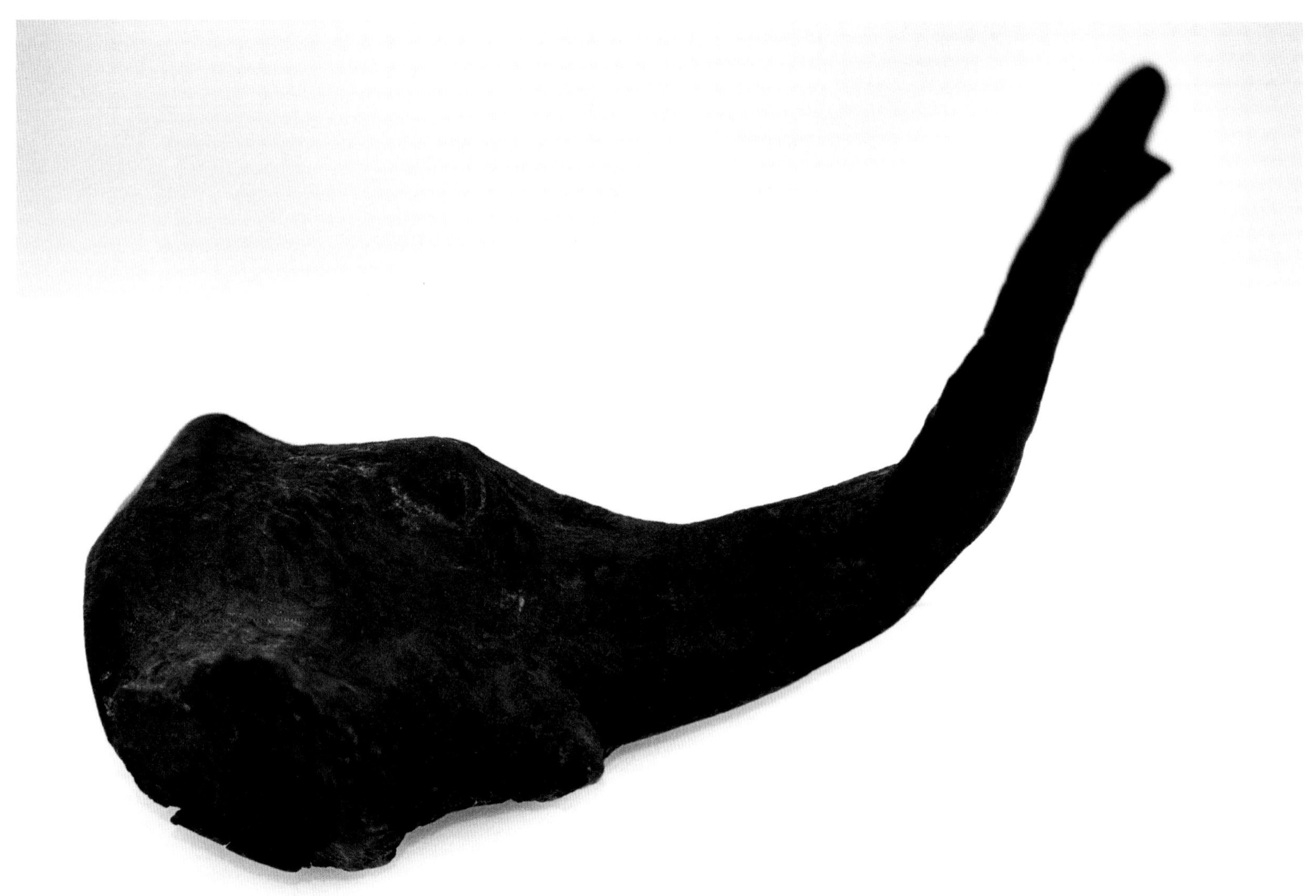

The Kitchen

A piece of driftwood in the shape of an elephant's head had been placed by Edward above the entrance door to the kitchen. It was perhaps the most striking elephant image in the house. Below the windows, which ran the length of the north side of the room, the countertop was covered with rocks. Being fond of Japanese literature and culture, Edward set about creating his own Zen rock garden. A selection of various oddly shaped colored rocks was carefully arranged. Some were stacked with a frog-shaped rock placed on top. Some had been placed in shallow bowls of water in order to maintain the color that had first attracted Edward when exploring the Cape seashore.

Although Edward frequently ate both breakfast and lunch at the nearby legendary eatery—Jack's Out Back—he was in fact a very capable cook. Not known as a social entertainer, he did host a few informal dinner parties while living at Elephant House. One of the parties had a rather unusual theme: Edward dyed each course of the dinner a shade of blue. At another dinner party, he was standing too close to the stove when his beard caught fire. It was quickly extinguished, and dinner went on, with Edward displaying a slightly thinner, curlier beard.

The kitchen was the room in which Edward usually met with people visiting the house. He often had a cup of tea with his guests at the small wooden table in the center of the room. Edward treasured the privacy of Elephant House. Few were invited to venture past this room. Edward usually met guests outside on the porch, or he waited with a book on a bench in the common across the way. He and his company would then depart to their destination. Elephant House remained for the most part Edward's private world.

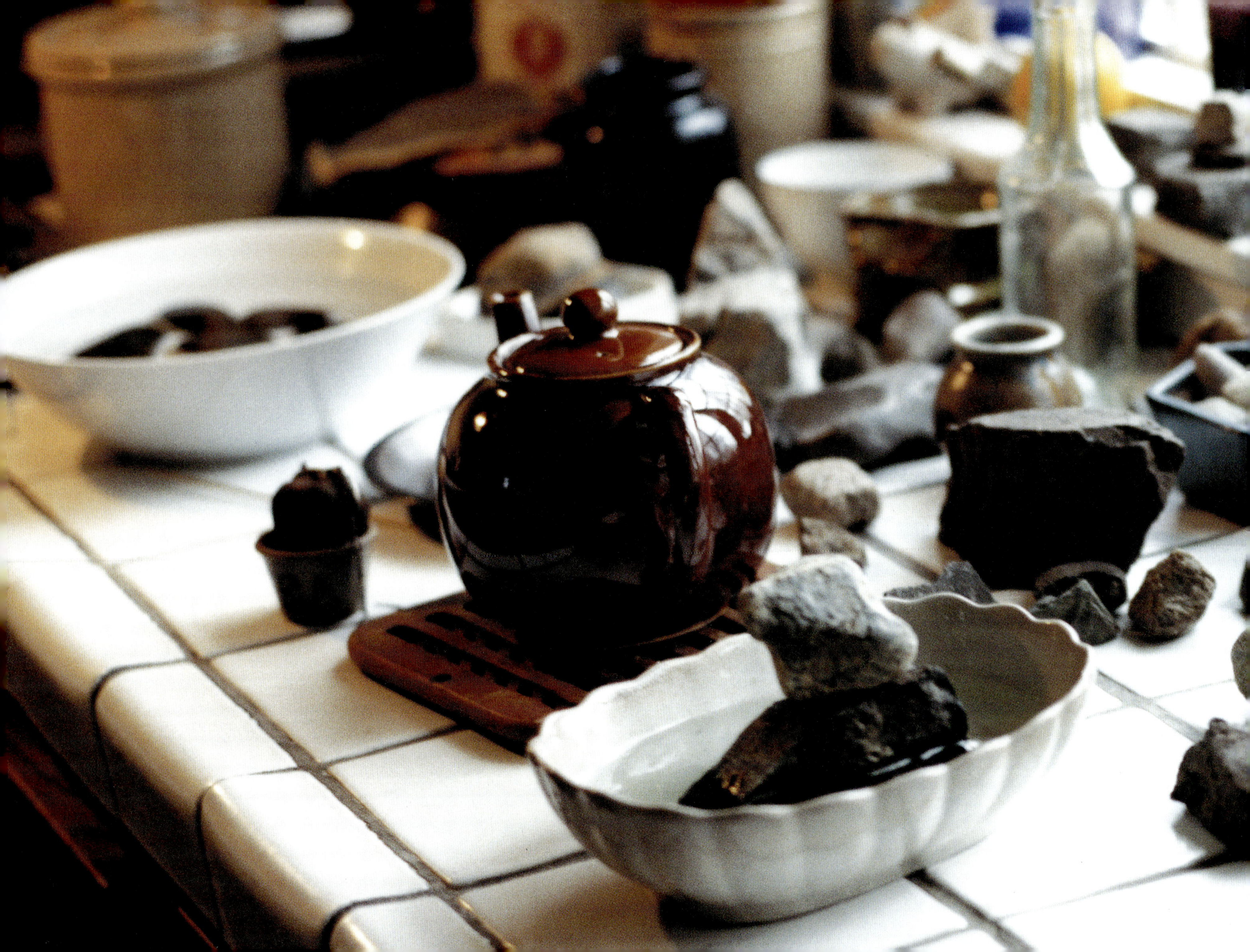

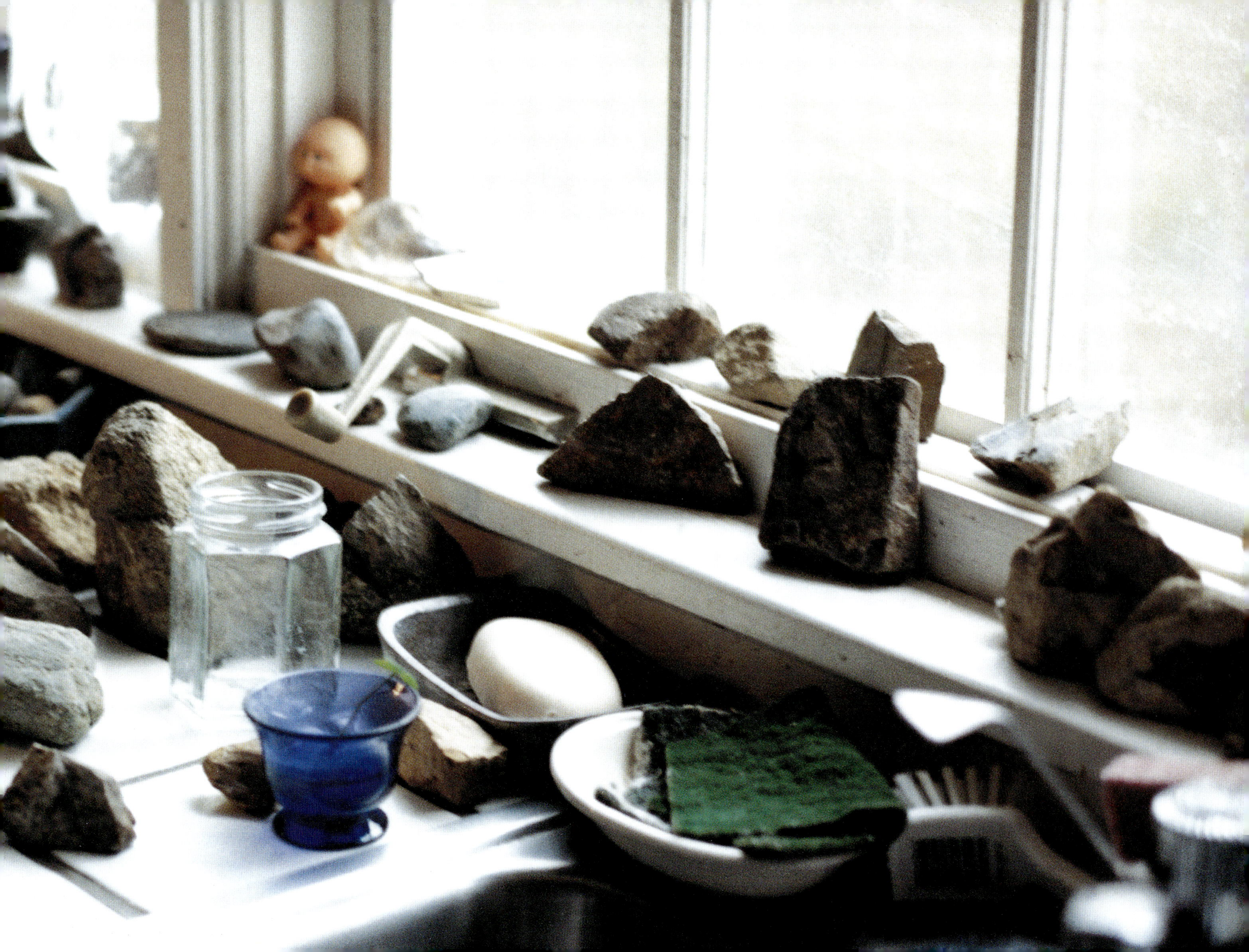

"[The House] really does need an awful lot of work, and if I got a large sum of money I would have it all fixed up - though I'm not sure I would have much of the inside fixed up more than it is. I rather like decay. I'm a little reluctant to take out a mortgage. Being free-lance, you never know."

—Edward Gorey, from "Edward Gorey and the Tao of Nonsense," Stephen Schiff, *The New Yorker*, Novermber 9, 1992

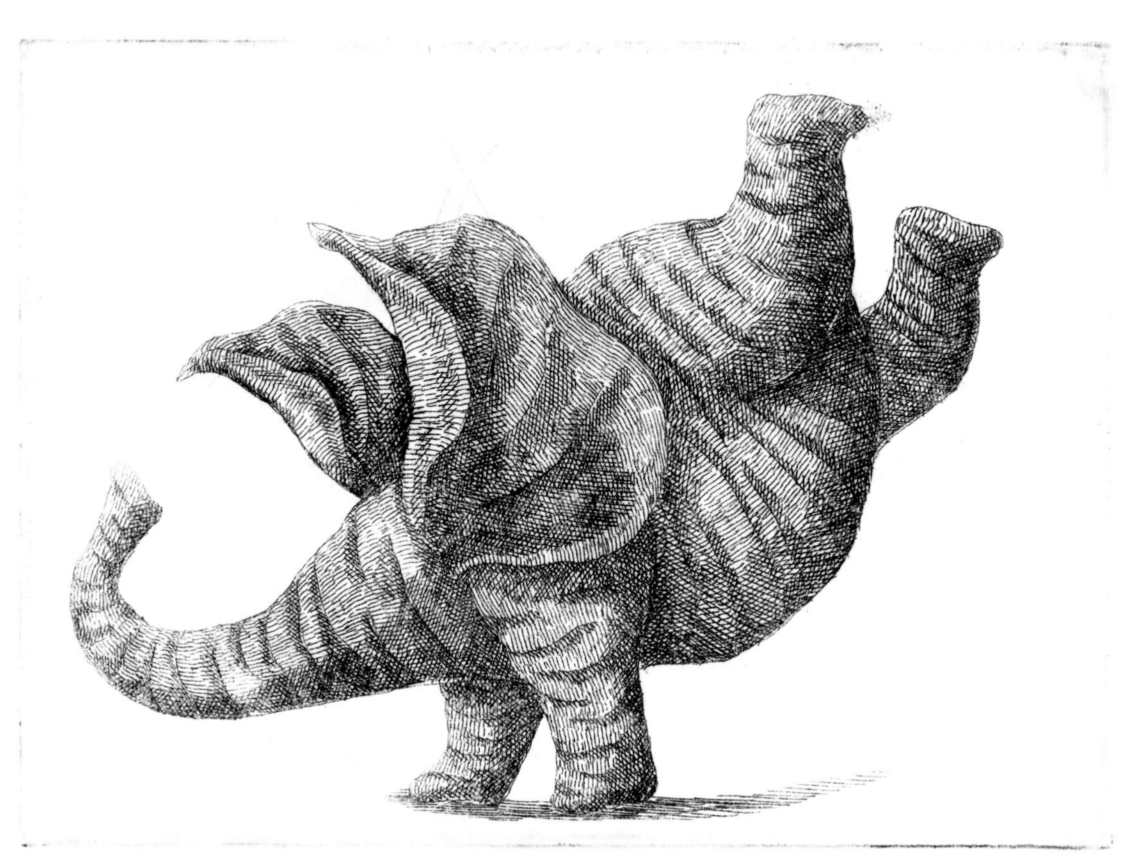

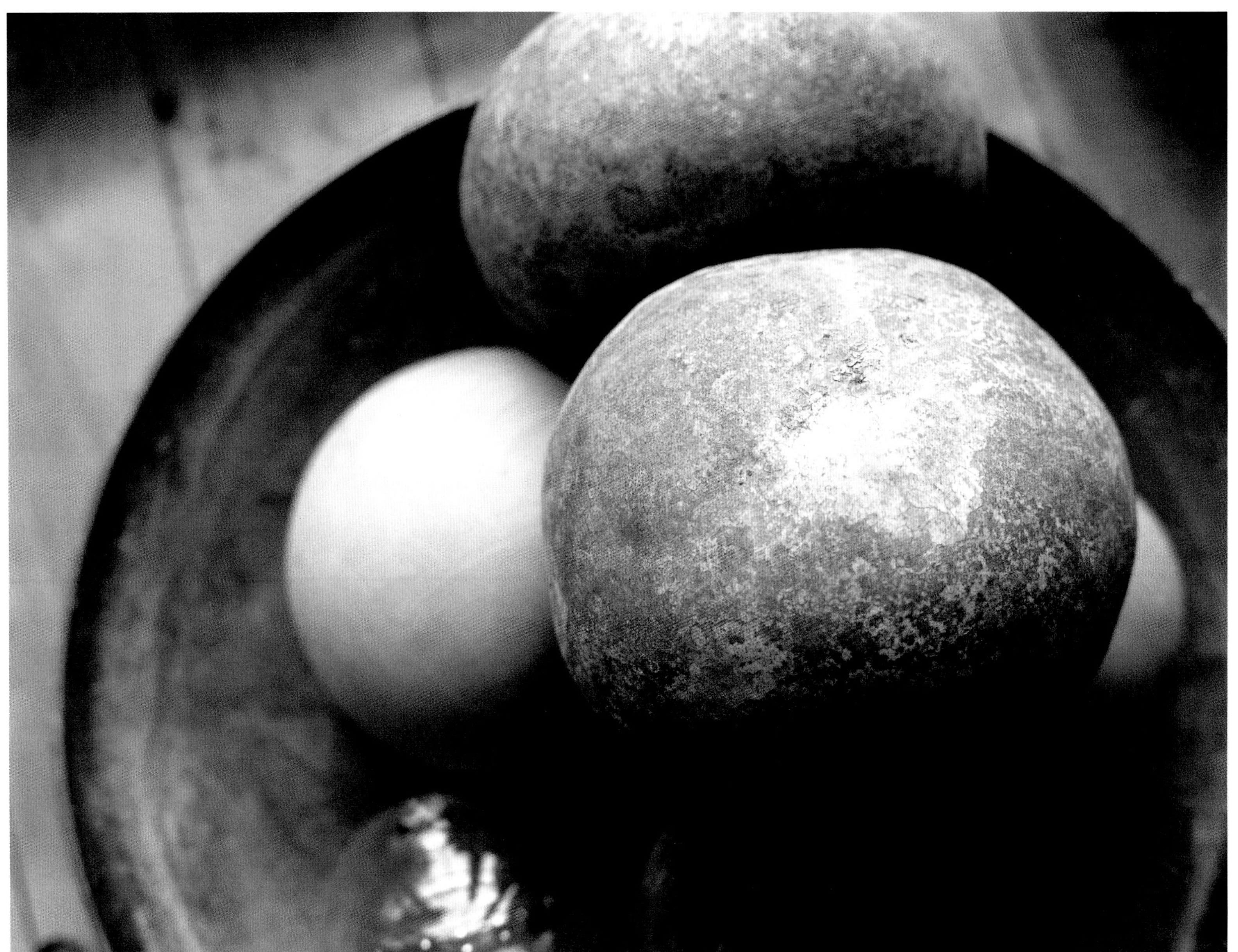

The Ball Room

Edward had a unique and often mysterious view of life. This back room on the first floor of the house acquired its name because of the many large and small glass, stone, wood, and composition balls that Edward set up as still lifes around the room. He covered the floor with these collections. He created a "city" of pewter salt and pepper shakers, tightly grouped on a tray and set on top of a stool. A nearby antique wood cupboard housed an extensive collection of Day of the Dead figures interspersed with old teapots. Edward's friend Lincoln Kirsten gave him an old porcelain cat playing with a ball. Set behind a wooden chair with a slatted back, the cat seemed to peer out from a cage. In the very center of these eclectic arrangements was his exercise bicycle, prescribed by his doctor and faithfully ridden by Edward. He would read a book as he pedaled, using the daylight from the large window.

Edward discovered a colony of raccoons had made their home in the window seat storage units of this room. They remained "in residence" for several years, and Edward chose not to dislodge them until they became a major problem.

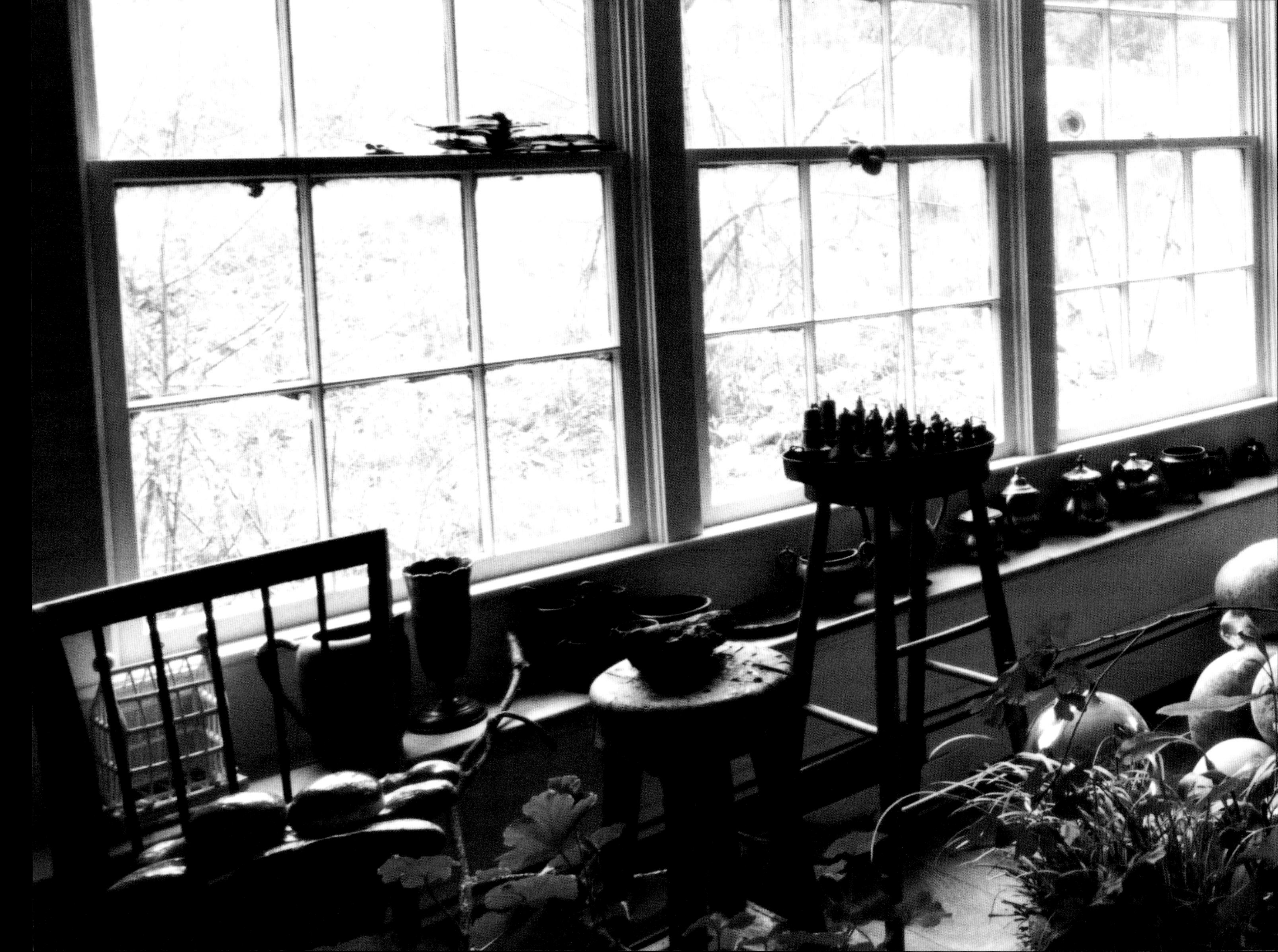

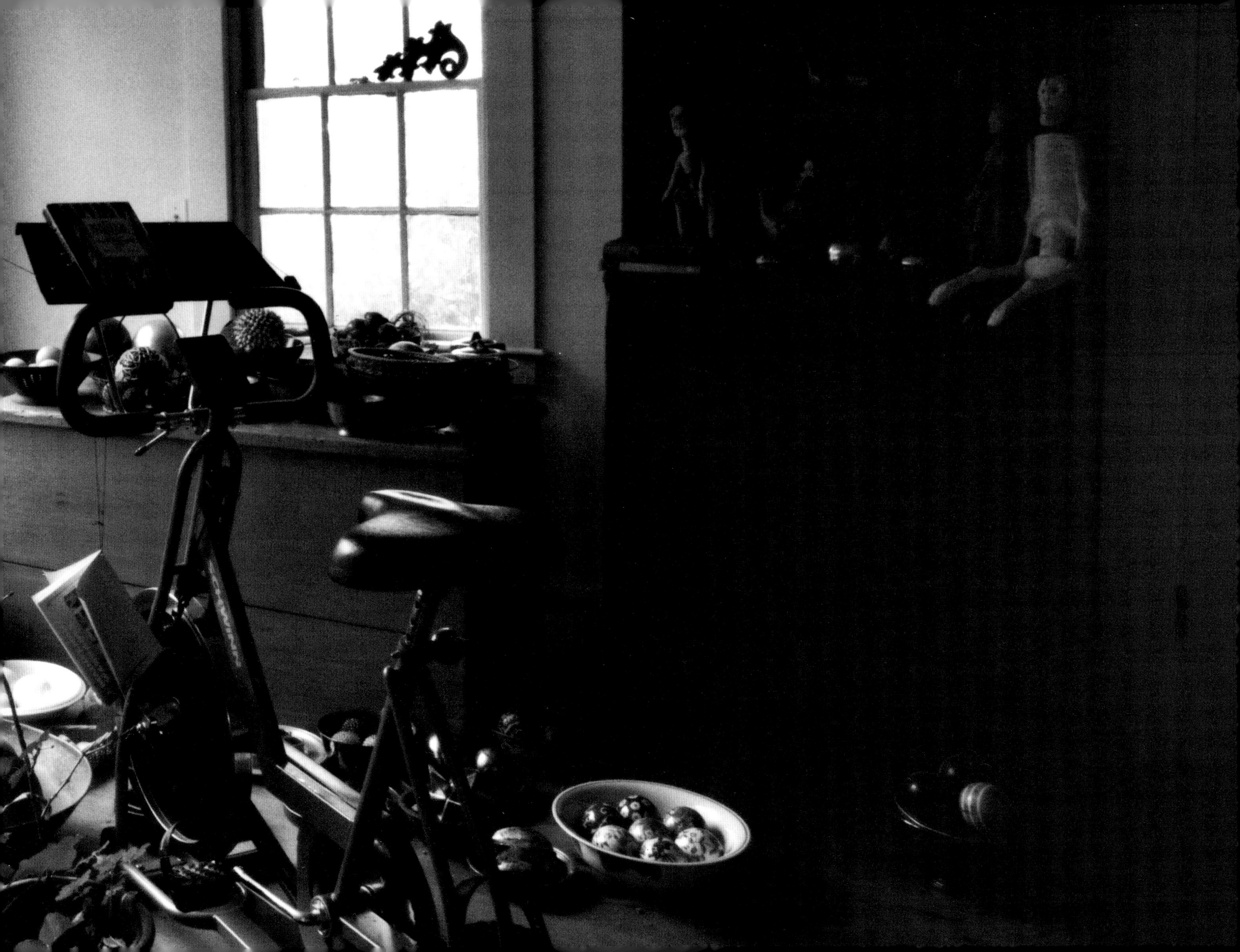

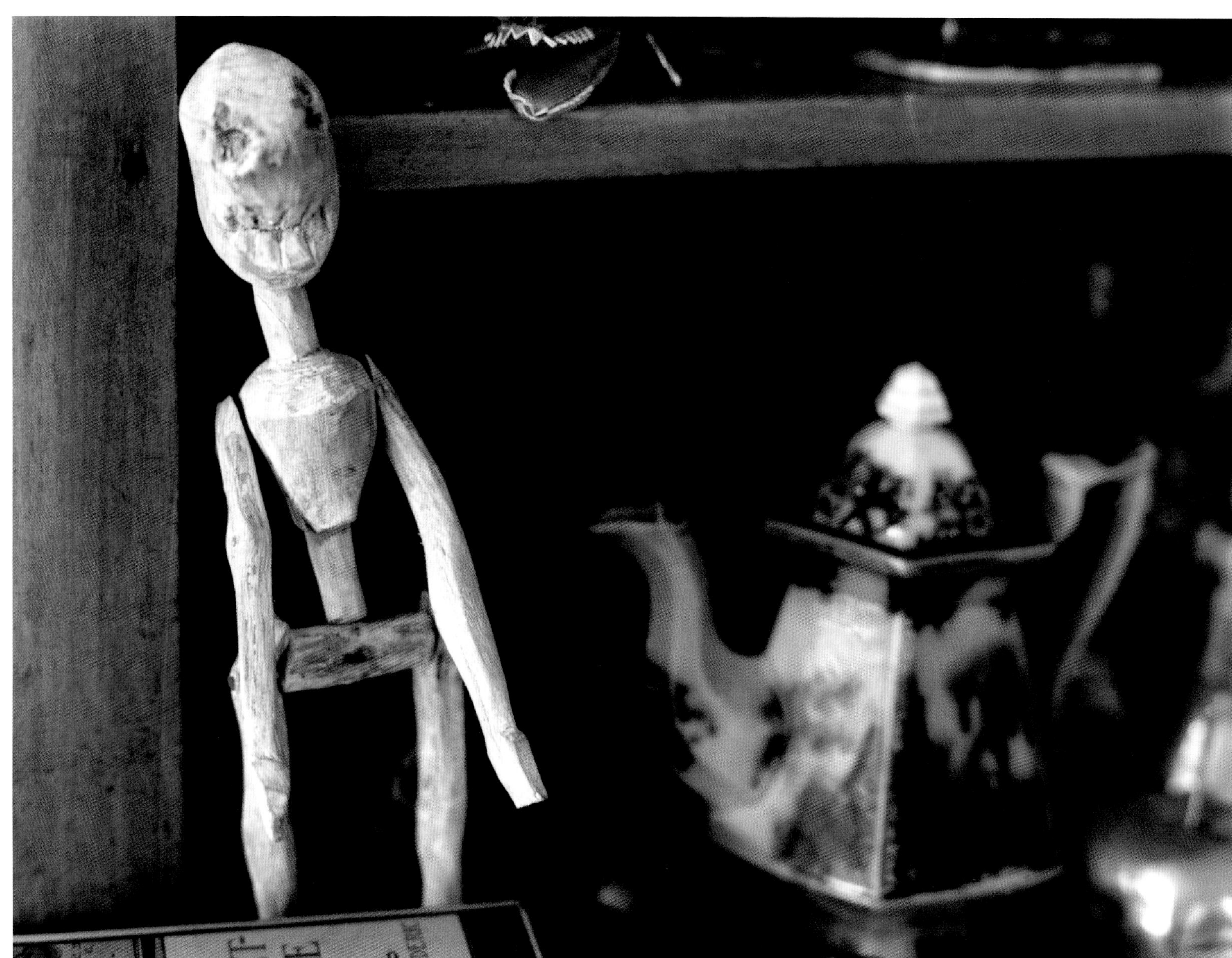

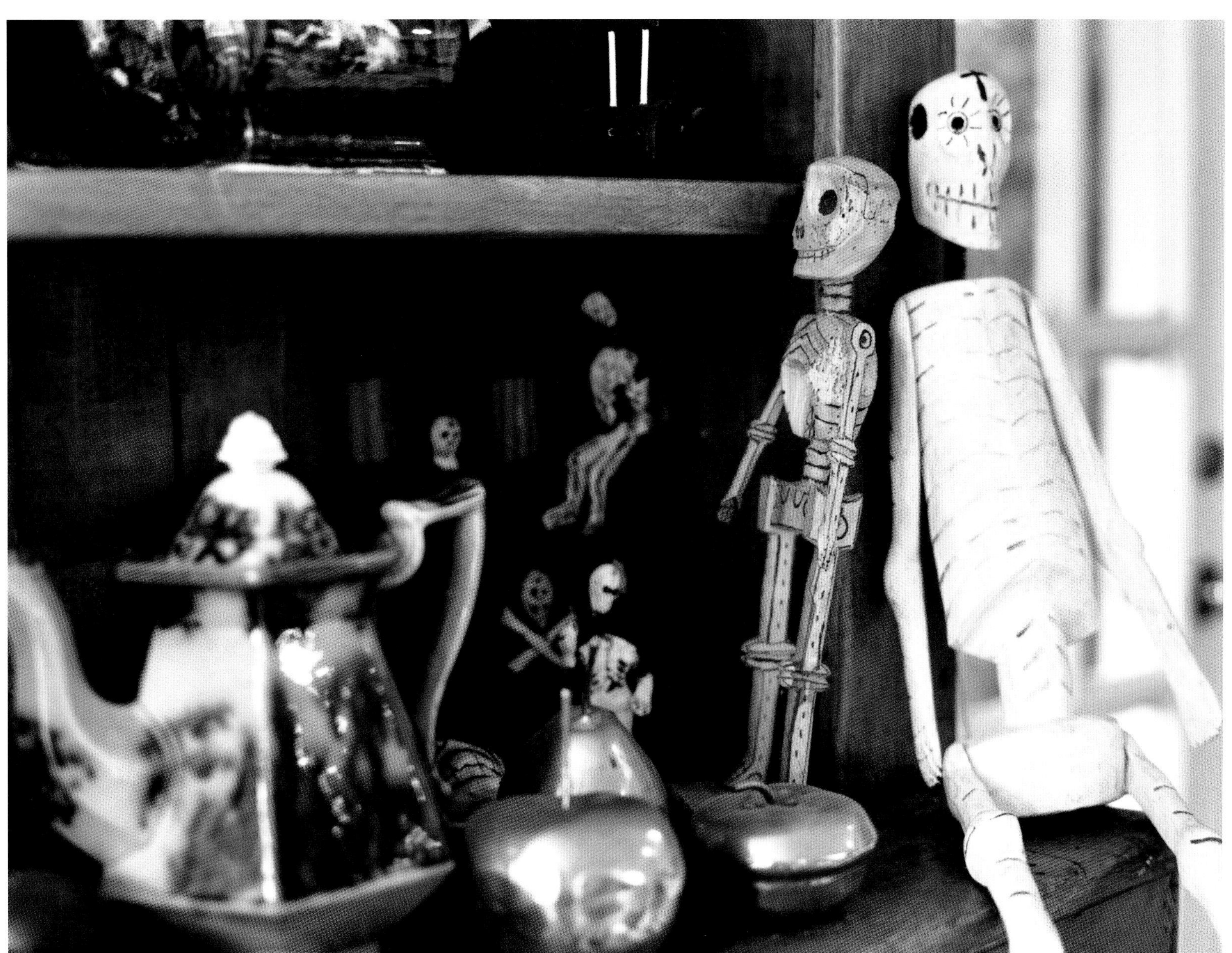

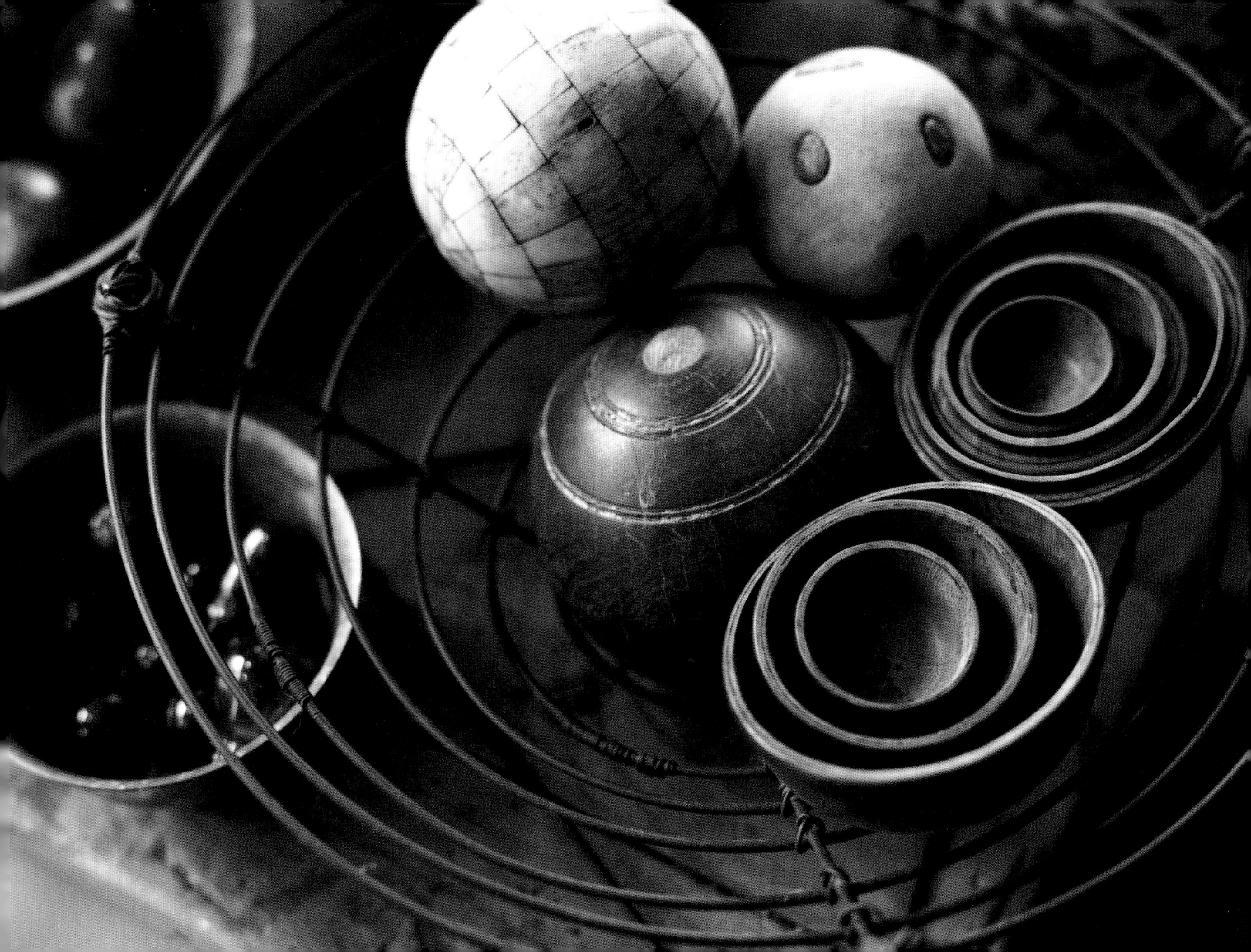

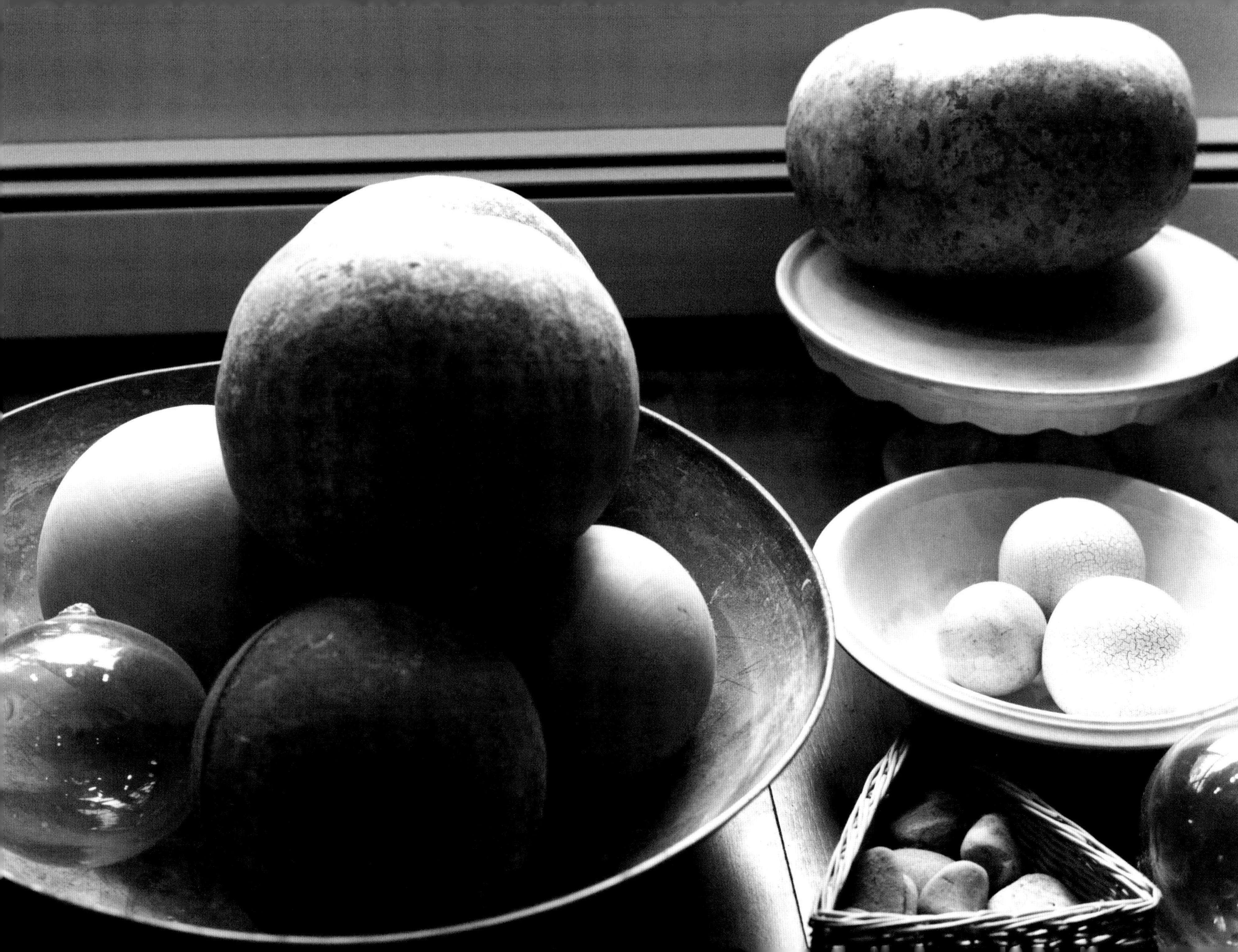

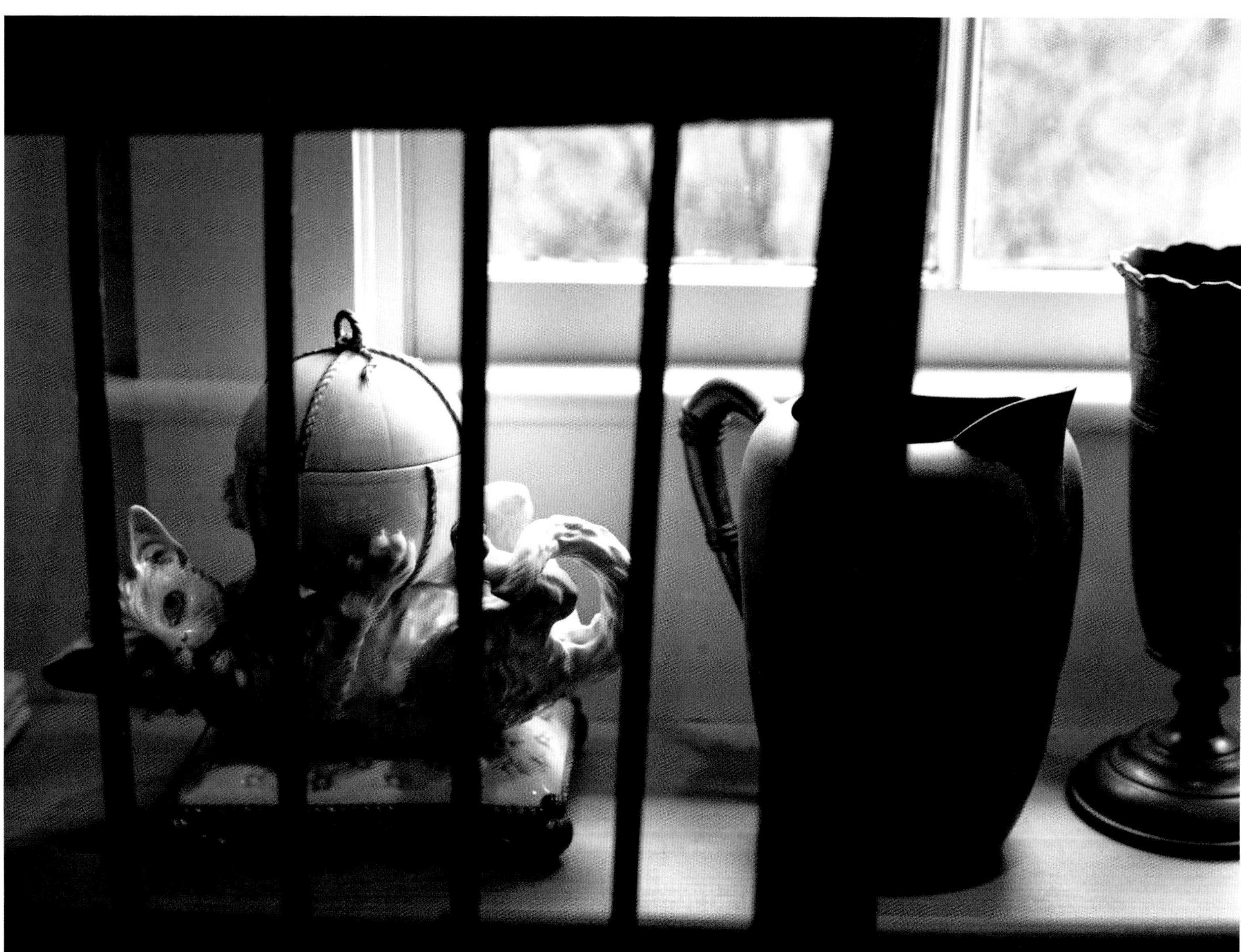

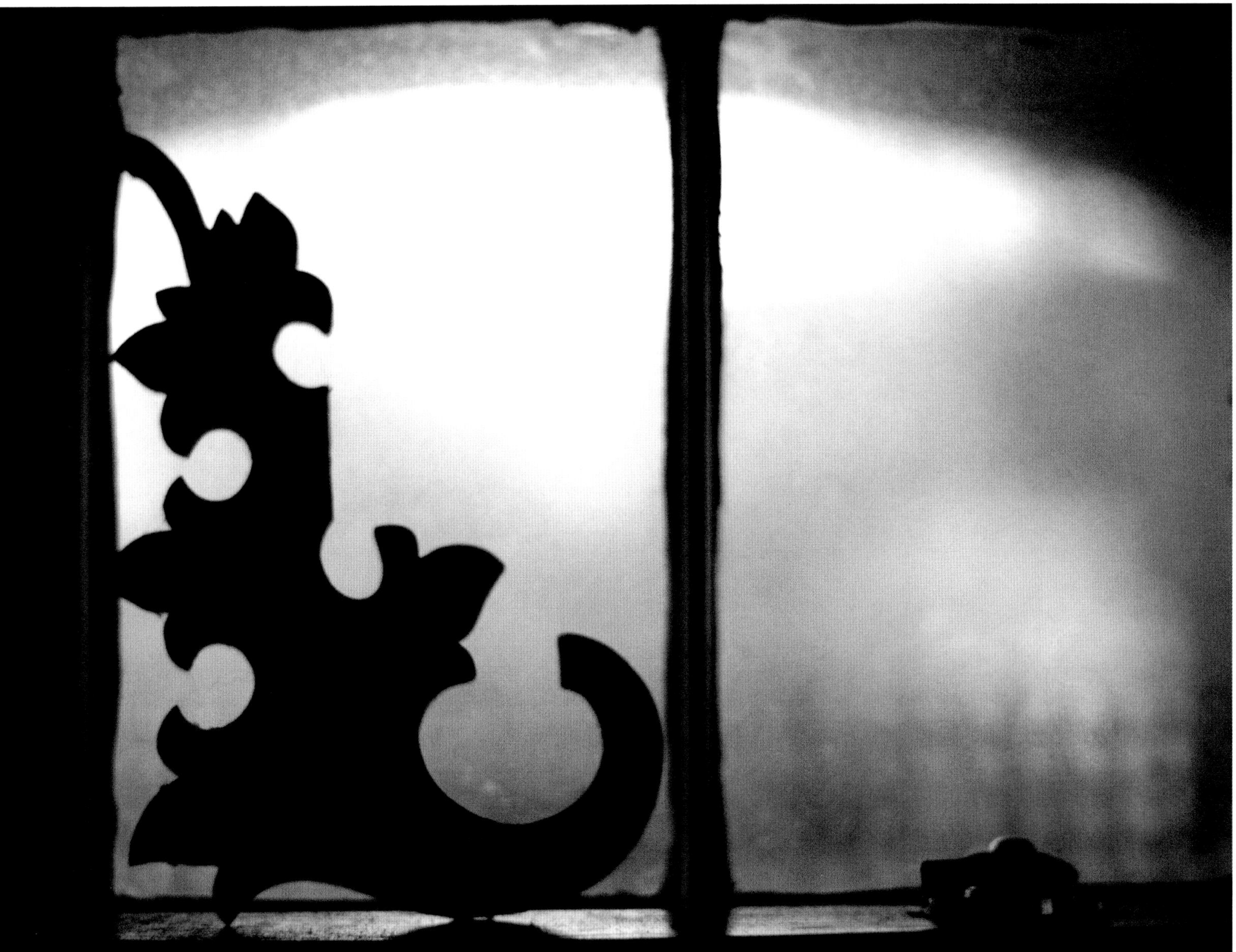

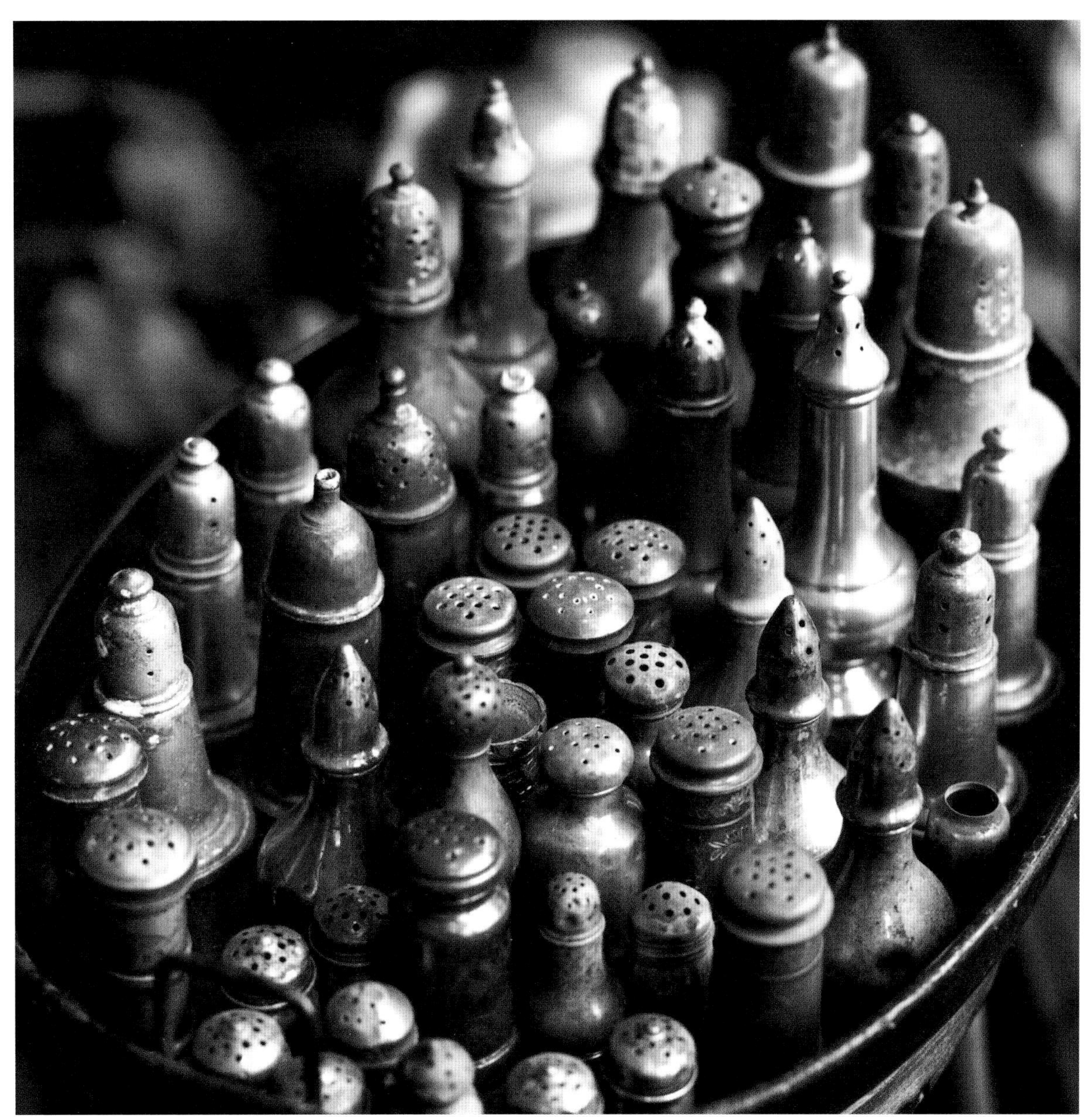

"If I'm working very hard, which is seldom, the last thing I want to do in order to relax is to be with people and babbling away and so forth. So I go to the movies or read a book or watch any of my thousands of tapes upstairs. Most of my friends in New York were my friends because we were all so busy going to things we had no time to do anything else. I might never have seen people if I didn't see them that way. Social events - foof. You know."

—Edward Gorey, from "Edward Gorey and the Tao of Nonsense," Stephen Schiff, *The New Yorker*, Novermber 9, 1992

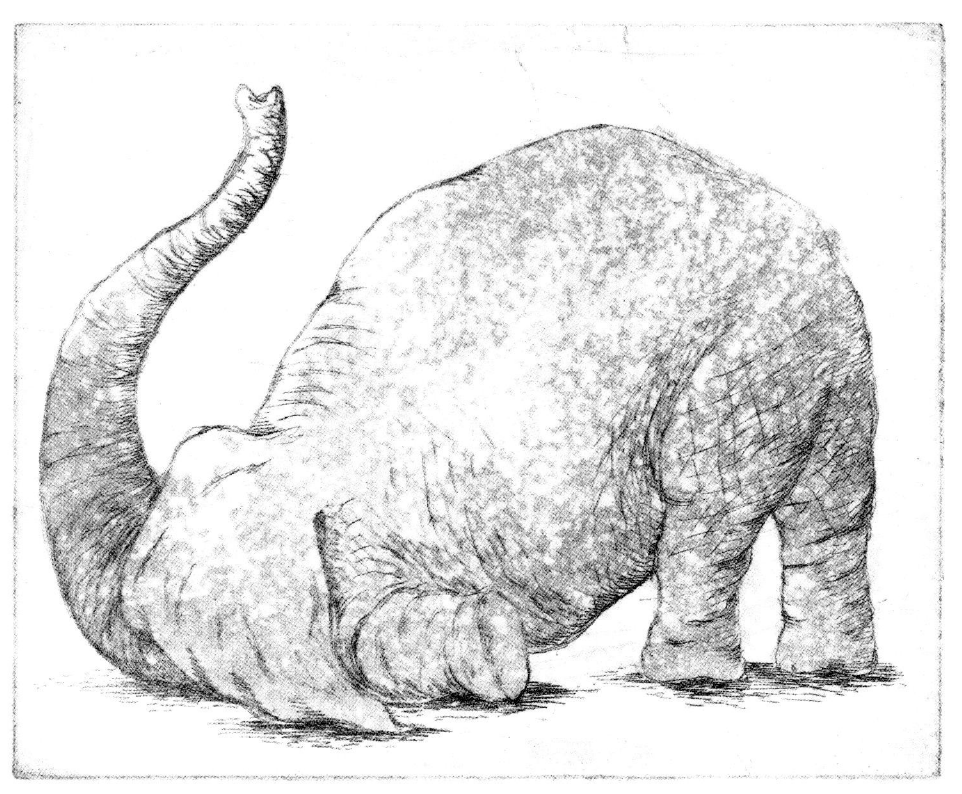

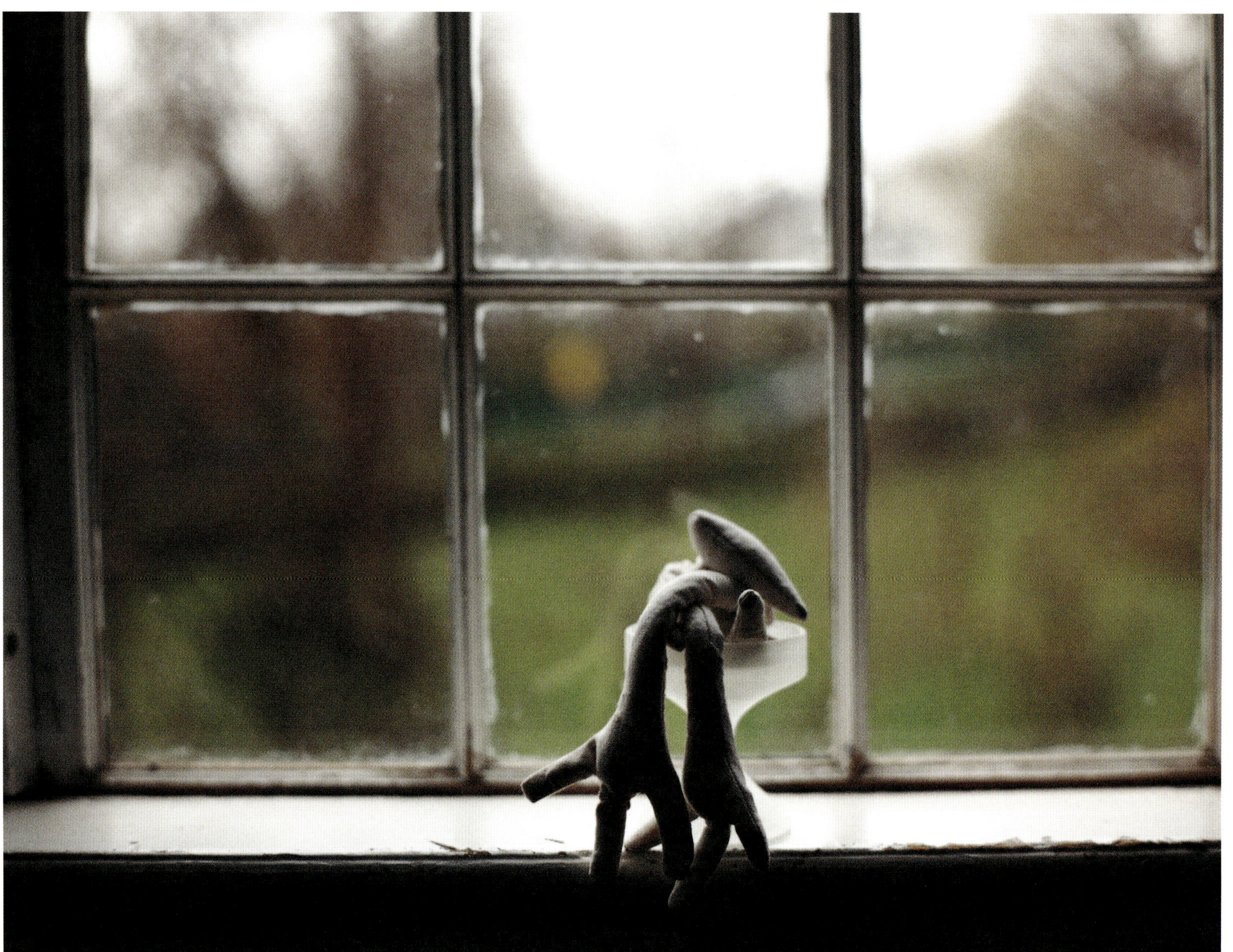

The Television Room

The steep narrow staircase next to the kitchen door led to a surprisingly large open-beamed space known as the television room. Other than his studio, this was the room where Edward spent most of his time. The combination of windows along the north wall and the skylights provided an abundance of light. Edward was a collector of culture. He created libraries of his favorite music and his favorite films and television shows. The walls were covered with shelves containing thousands of books, record albums, cassettes, CDs, VHS tapes, miscellaneous collectibles, magazines, and newspapers. He had so many CDs that more than a few were still in their plastic wrapping. His collection was filled with the music of Bach, Beethoven, and the twentieth-century French composer Erik Satie. He joined music clubs by mail, and, being particularly fond of baroque music, once ordered all the baroque music listings featured in a catalog. Over the years Edward acquired an extensive collection of rarely performed Haydn, Handel, and Mozart operas—Mozart was a hero of Edward's.

Edward's taste in television was eclectic. Among his favorites were *The Mary Tyler Moore Show, The Golden Girls, Third Rock from the Sun, Frasier, The X-Files,* and *Buffy the Vampire Slayer*. He would sit on the couch, watch television, and sew Figbash dolls (one of the characters from *The Raging Tide,* which captivated Edward the rest of his life). Being a collector, he videotaped his favorite shows. He began with Betamax (*The Golden Girls* were on Beta) and switched over to VHS. He taped every episode of *Buffy*. On the sofa were seven or eight television guides: one for the satellite dish, one for the cable, one for local programs, etc. He knitted a small, pocketed remote control holder to house the many remotes. Edward feigned not being able to do the simplest household chore, but he could program the VCR to switch taping from cable to satellite on West Coast time. Each tape had the program title, a Roman numeral, and the date and time the episode aired.

Edward's cats could be quite adventurous. One evening, his cat Thomas knocked over the television. The cats would literally bounce off the wall behind the television and jump onto the crossbeams. They left permanent paw prints on the wall. On this occasion Thomas misjudged the distance, and the television came crashing to the floor.

In the area surrounding the sofa were boxes of opened and unopened mail, much of it from fans. To cope with this ever-increasing tidal wave of incoming mail, Edward designed his own postcard reply, which read, "You've written me to no avail, because I never read my mail." It depicted a very large urn overflowing with correspondence and a cat napping on top of the pile. However, even a postcard reply from Edward was rare.

Edward suffered his fatal heart attack in this room. He was sitting on the couch while his friend Rick Jones was replacing the battery of the telephone a few feet away. Rick heard a gasp from Edward. It was instantaneous: he had the attack and collapsed. The paramedics arrived quickly and began efforts to resuscitate Edward. After an hour they were successful in reestablishing vital signs. Edward was kept alive on life support for three days at the hospital. He was pronounced dead on April 15, 2000.

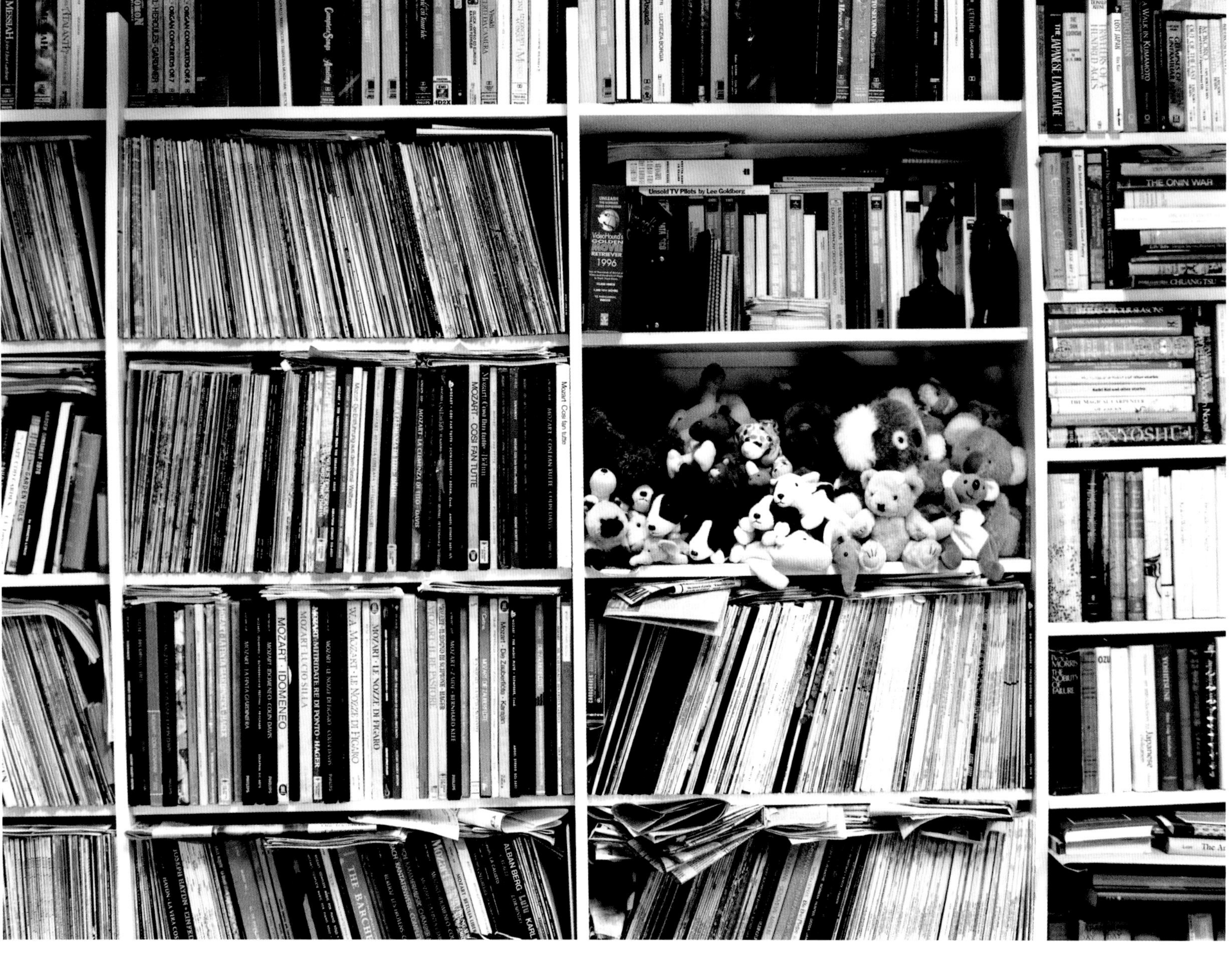
MESSIAH
THE JAPANESE LANGUAGE
A WALK IN KUMAMOTO
LUCREZIA BORGIA
Unsold TV Pilots by Lee Goldberg
VideoHound's GOLDEN MOVIE RETRIEVER 1996
THE ONIN WAR
CHUANG TSU
MOZART · COSI FAN TUTTE
MOZART · IDOMENEO
MOZART · LE NOZZE DI FIGARO
ALBAN BERG
THE NOBILITY OF FAILURE
OZU

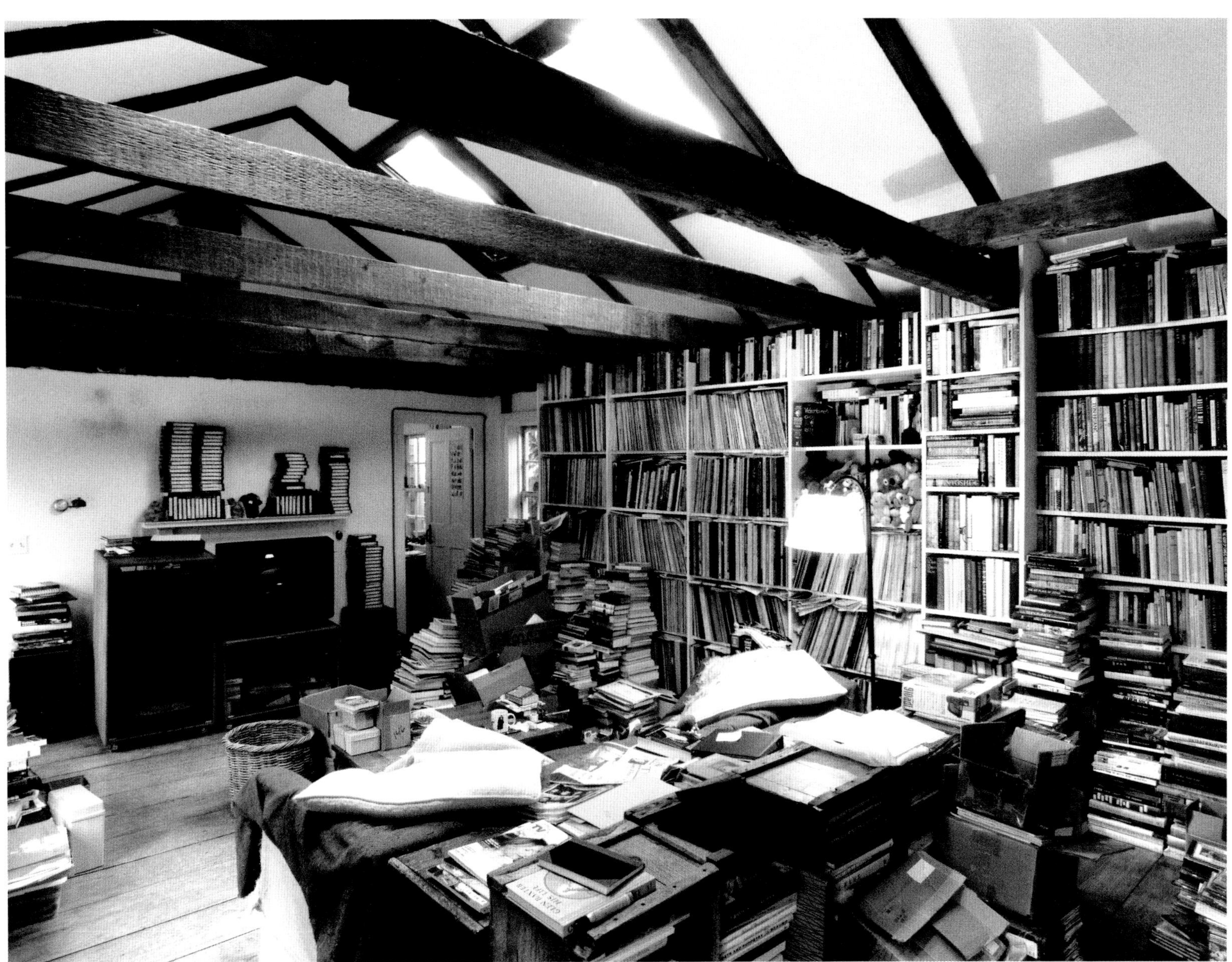

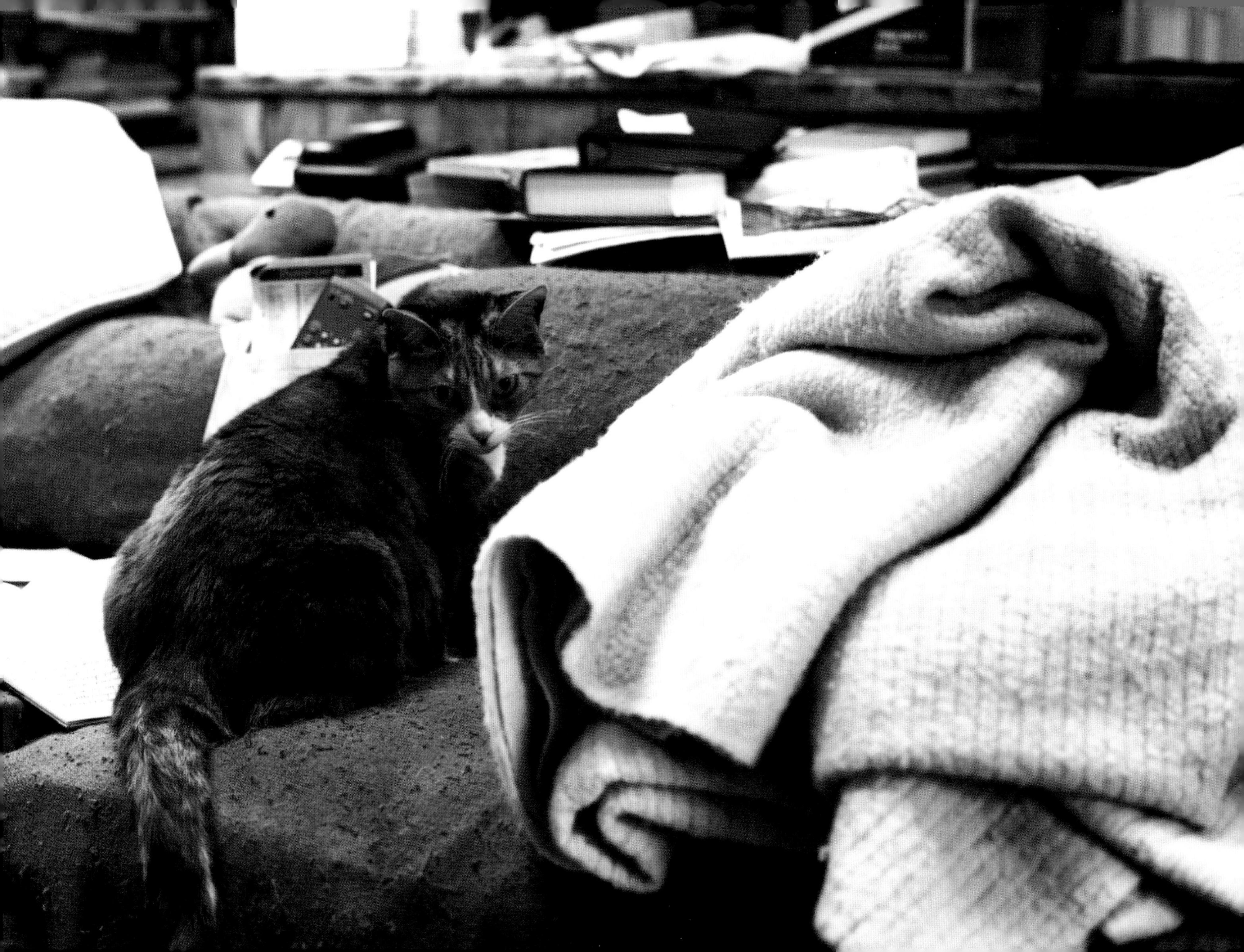

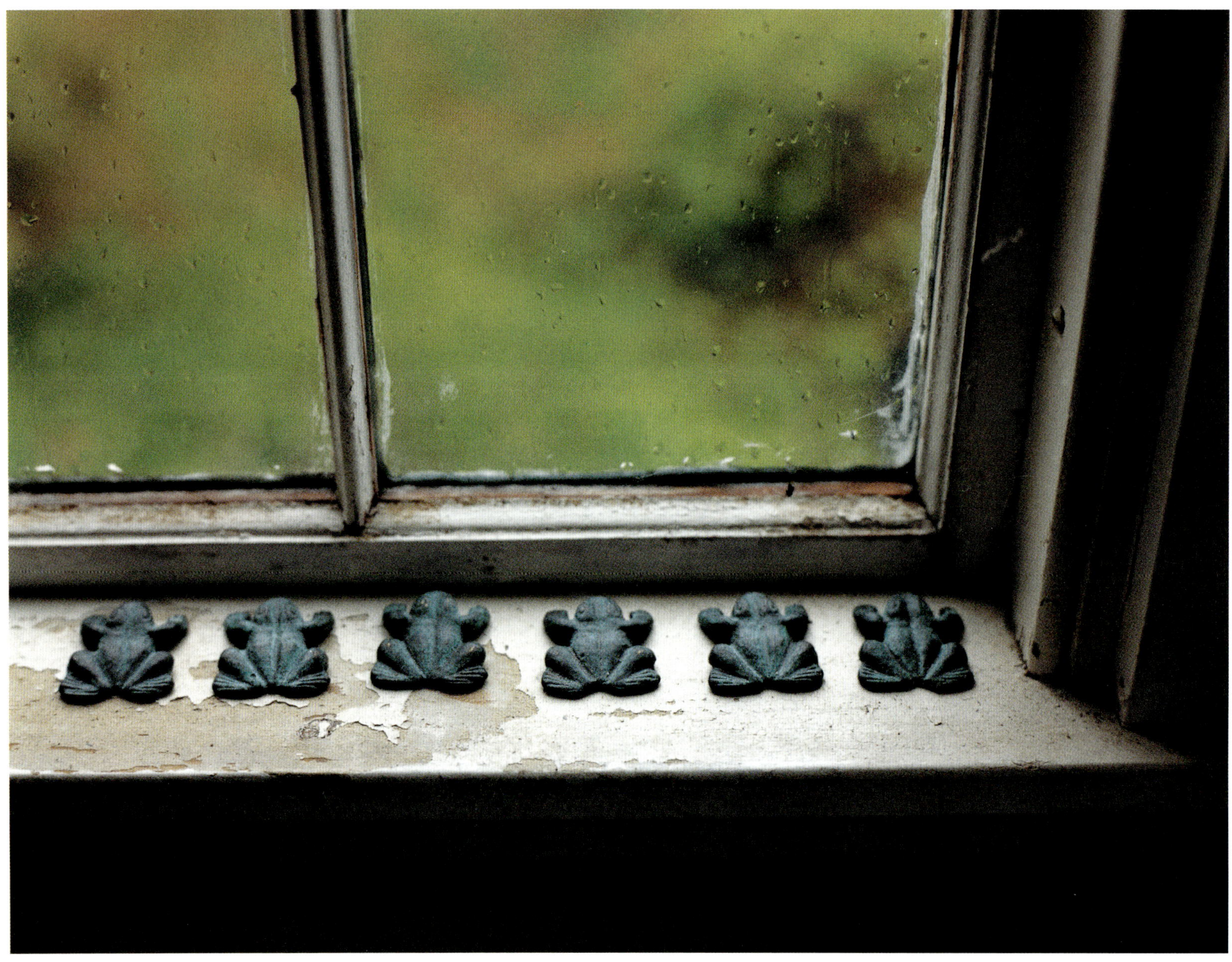

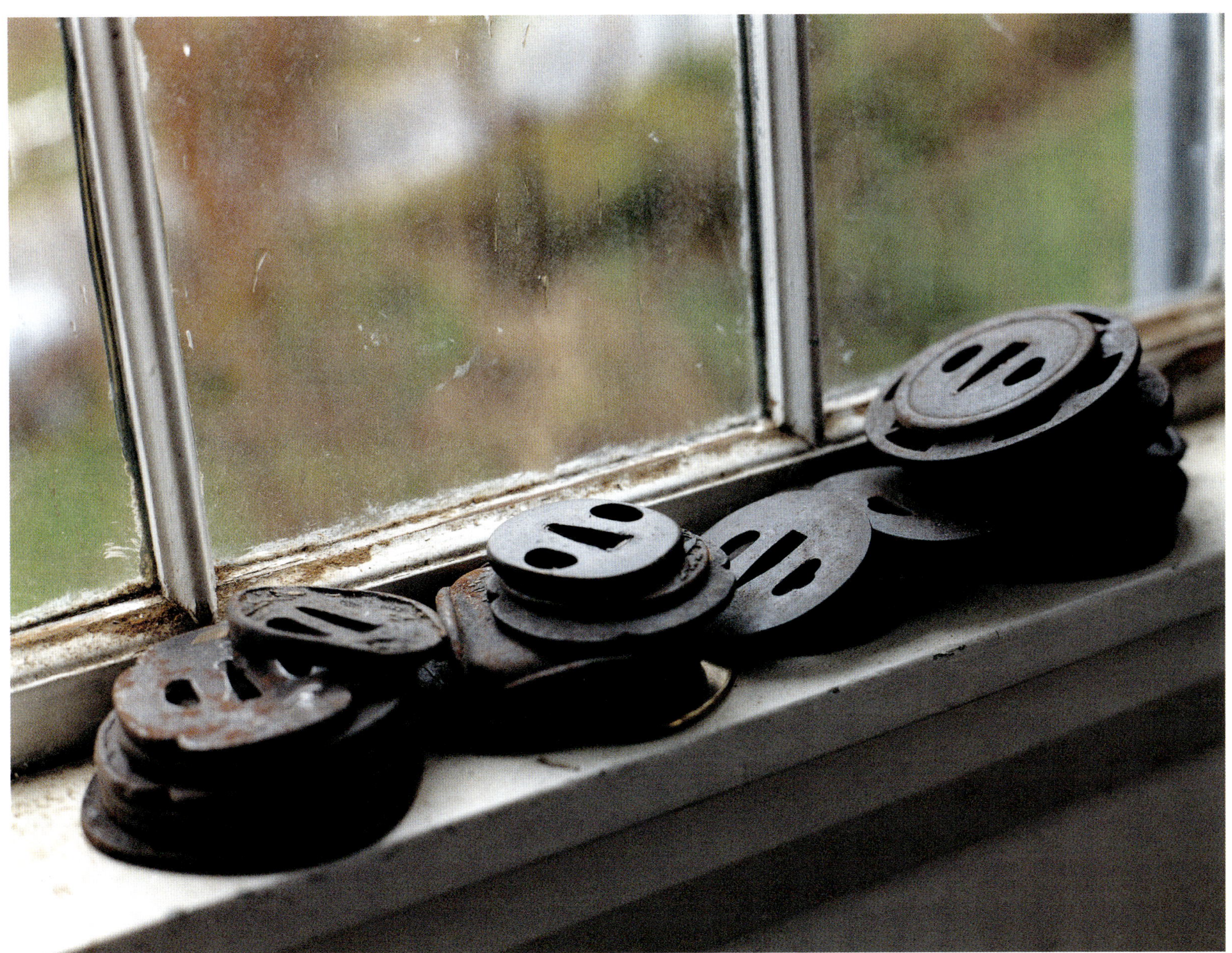

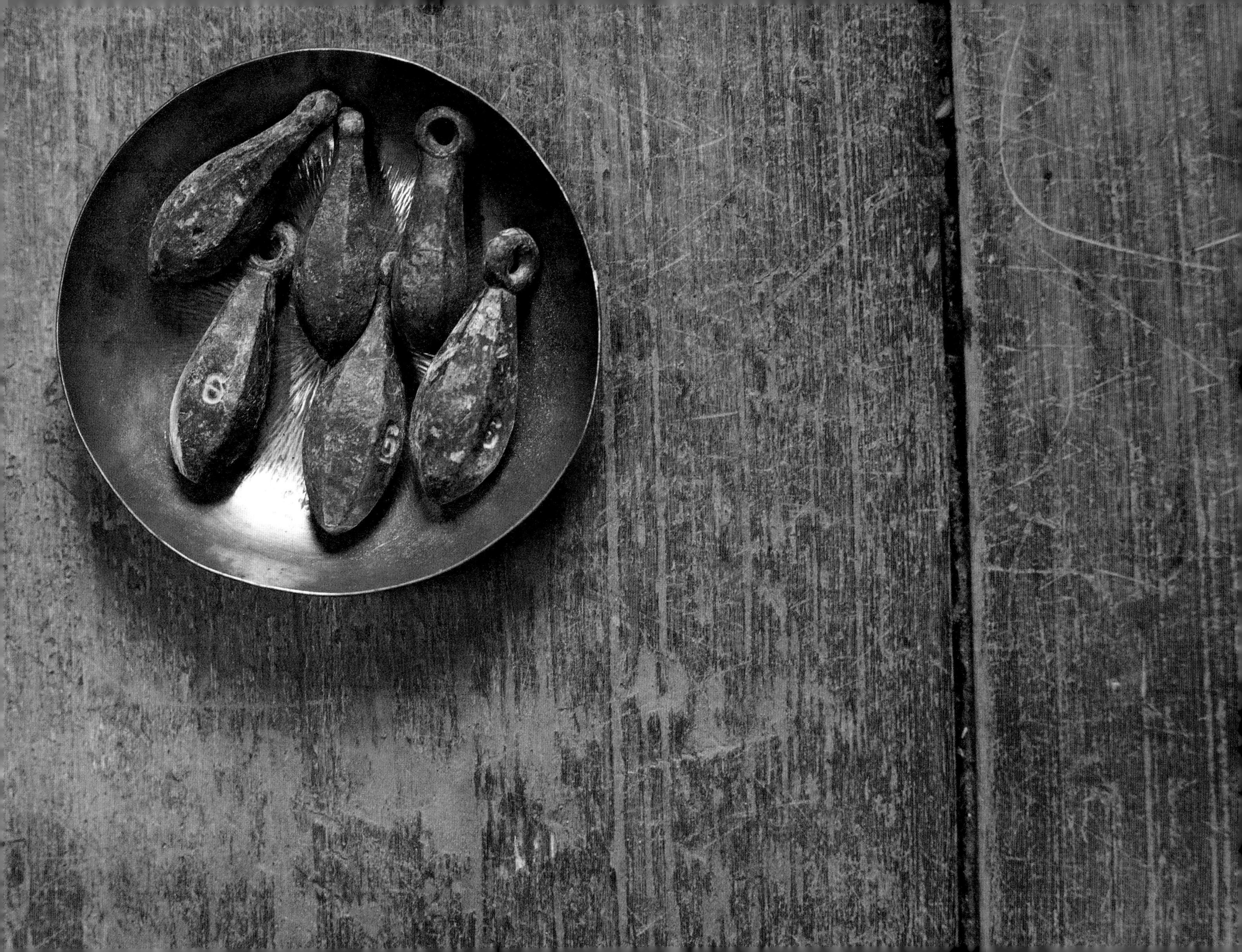

For writing Mr Earbrass affects an athletic sweater of forgotten origin and unknown significance; it is always worn hind-side-to.

—Edward Gorey, from *The Unstrung Harp: or, Mr Earbrass Writes a Novel*

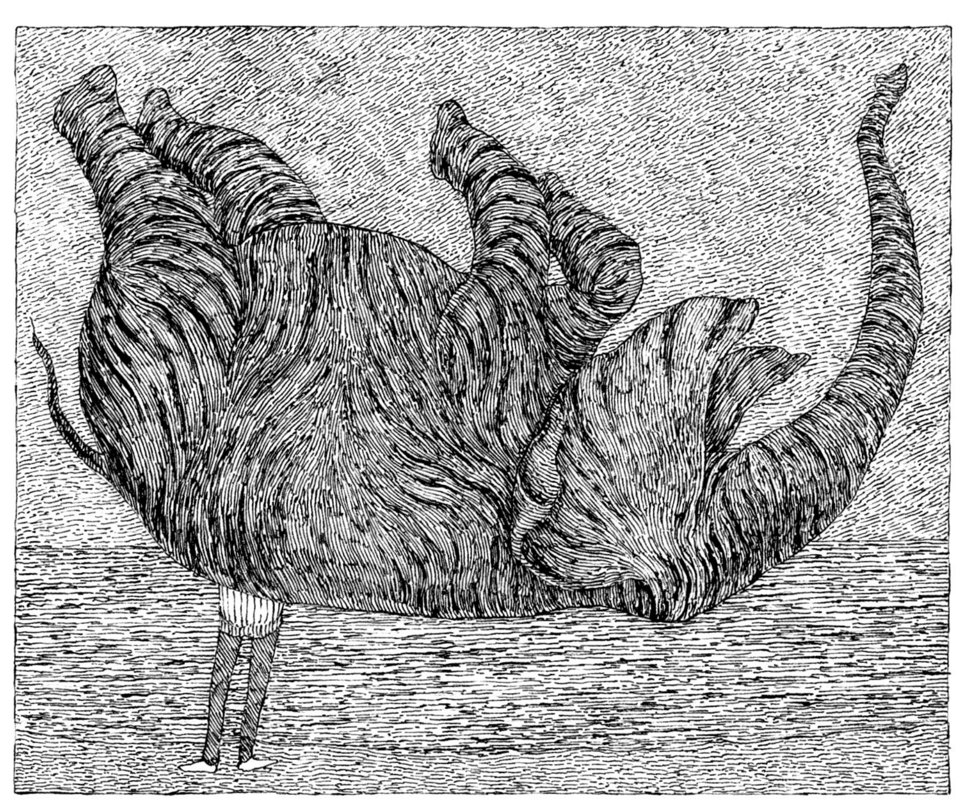

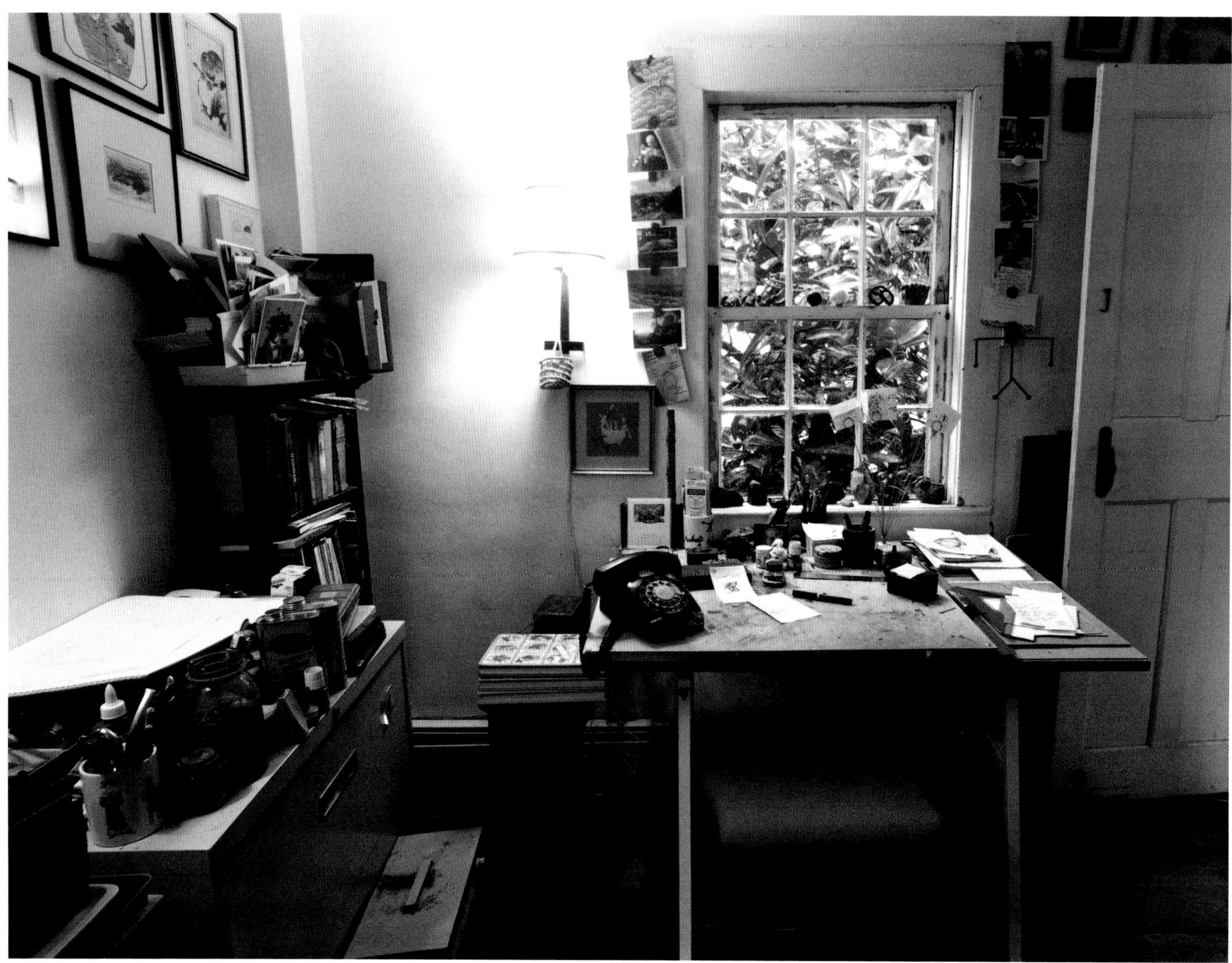

The Studio

Directly off the television room was Edward's studio. In all the other rooms in the house one could look out at the world, but in this very small room Edward created a workplace with only one window, which faced directly into the dense upper branches of his beloved magnolia tree. He did not want distraction. Although he often stated that he "dithered," it is clear from the massive amount of artwork he completed (some eight to ten thousand images) that he was in fact highly disciplined. During the early years of his professional life he often committed himself to more work deadlines than he could meet. While living with his family at Mill Way, when the telephone rang, the person answering the phone would turn to Edward and ask, "Are you home?" before picking up the receiver. He was not fond of deadlines.

While working at his drawing board, Edward permitted his cats to roam in and out of the room. On more than one occasion cats would decide to join Edward at the board, which led to a number of unfortunate results. Edward's Taoist philosophy resulted in extreme tolerance of the cats' conduct. His archives contain more than one example of a dried puddle of spilled ink destroying a large, complex crosshatched drawing. While working, Edward used an ergonomically correct kneeling chair to help support his lower back. From this kneeling position, he could easily reach nearby files without having to get up from the chair. It is amazing to realize that from that position, on such a small table, the brilliance of Edward's world came to life.

45 STREET, NEW YORK • MU 7-105
MADE IN U.S.A.
HUXLEY HOUSE
WORLDWIDE TREASURE BUREAU
P.O. Box 5012 • Visalia, CA 93278-5012

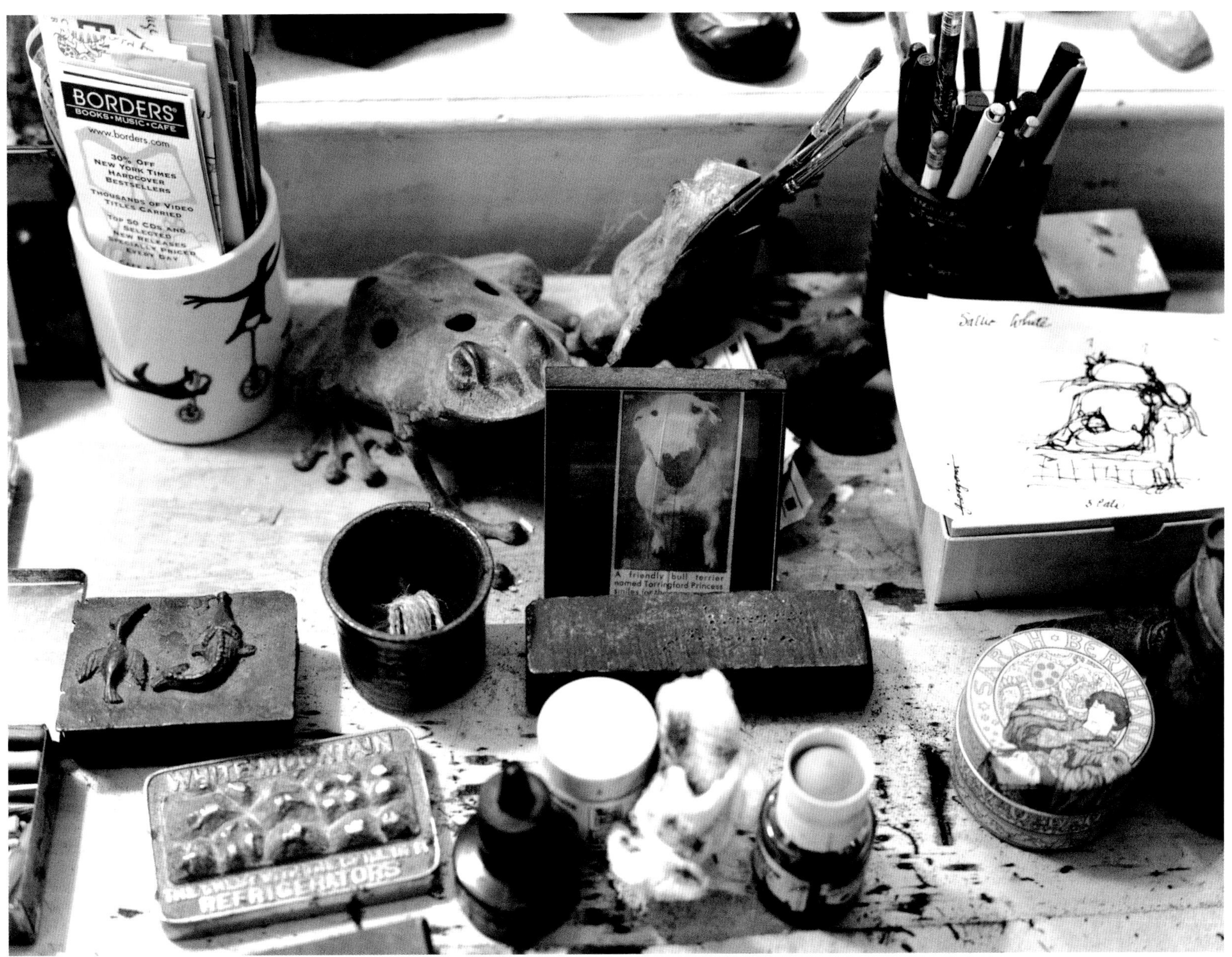
BORDERS®
BOOKS•MUSIC•CAFE
www.borders.com
30% OFF
NEW YORK TIMES
HARDCOVER
BESTSELLERS
THOUSANDS OF VIDEO
TITLES CARRIED
A friendly bull terrier
named Torringford Princess
WHITE MOUNTAIN
REFRIGERATORS
SARAH BERNHA

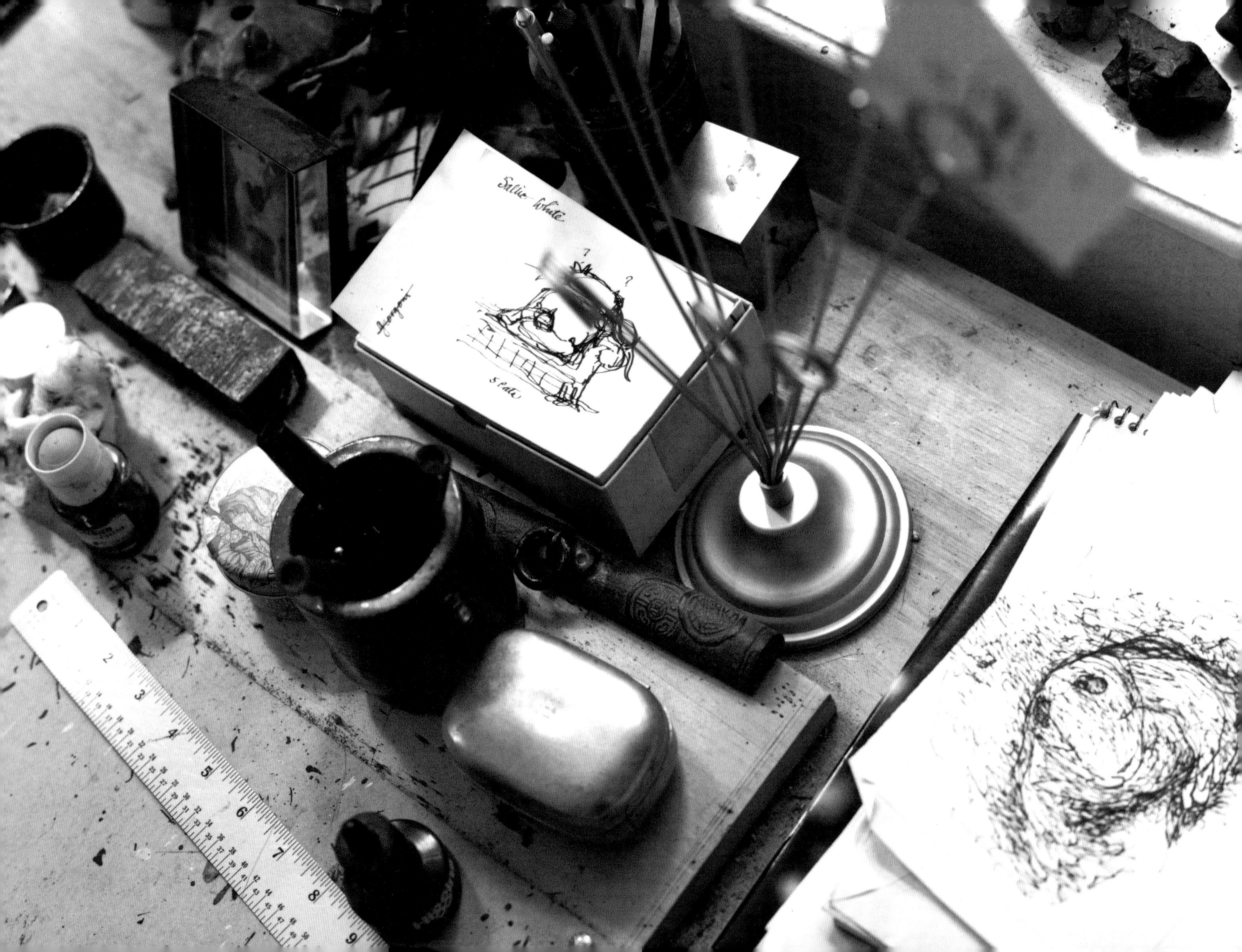
Sallie White

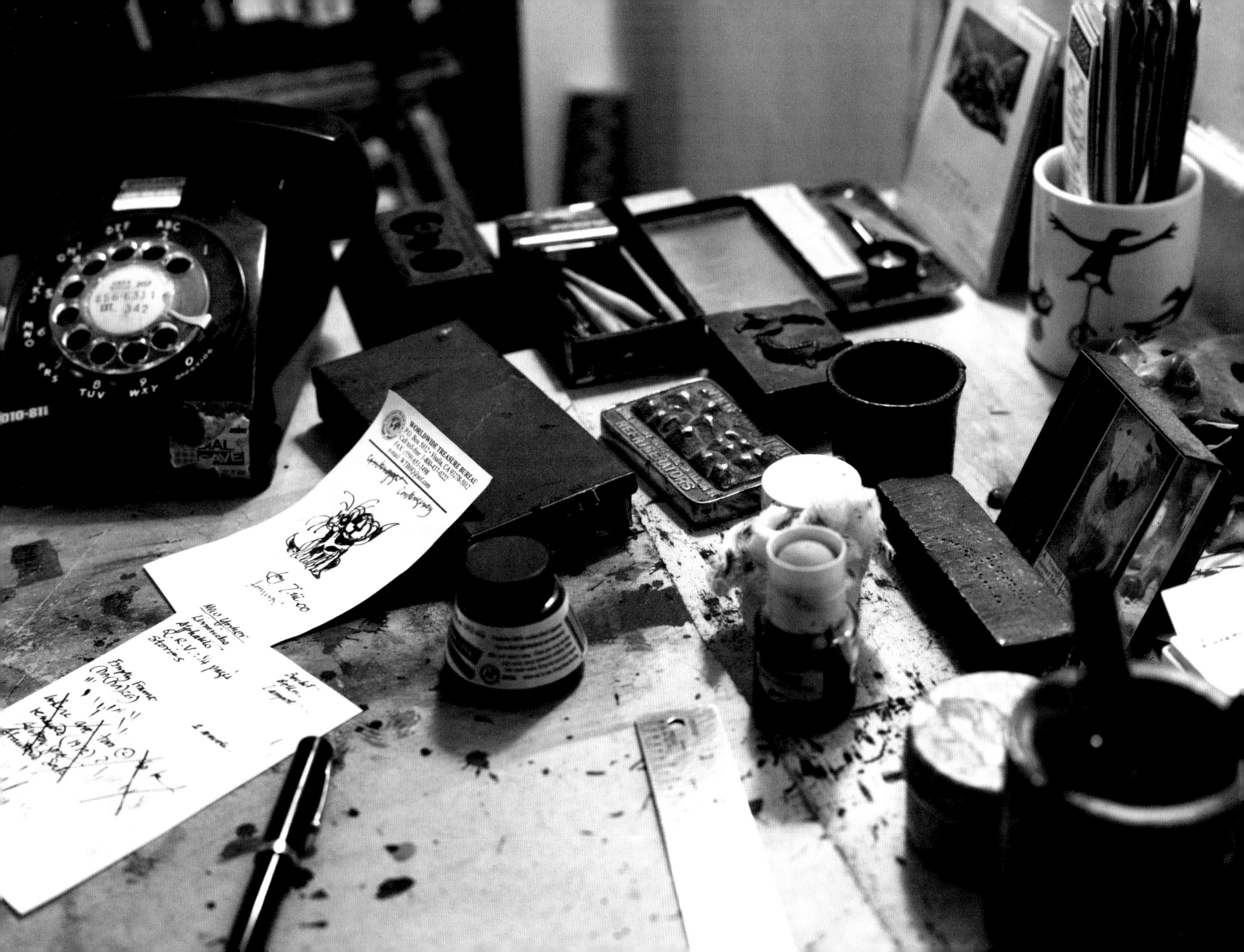
WORLDWIDE TREASURE BUREAU
P.O. Box 5012 • Visalia, CA 93278-5012
Call toll-free 1-800-437-0222
FAX (559) 651-3498
e-mail: WTBHQ@aol.com

Mr. Oswell's shock at finding them together in the bathtub having proved fatal, Larry and Freddie were free to be married by a sympathetic clergyman in Niantic, Connecticut.

She did not, after all, lose her toes to frostbite, and, in the spring in St. Petersburg, received a standing ovation for her thirty-two quadruple fouettés at the end of Act IV of Zerapilla.

So at last, after an unbelievable number of vicissitudes and disasters, Sophia Charlotte was restored to her parents.

—Edward Gorey, from *The Happy Ending*

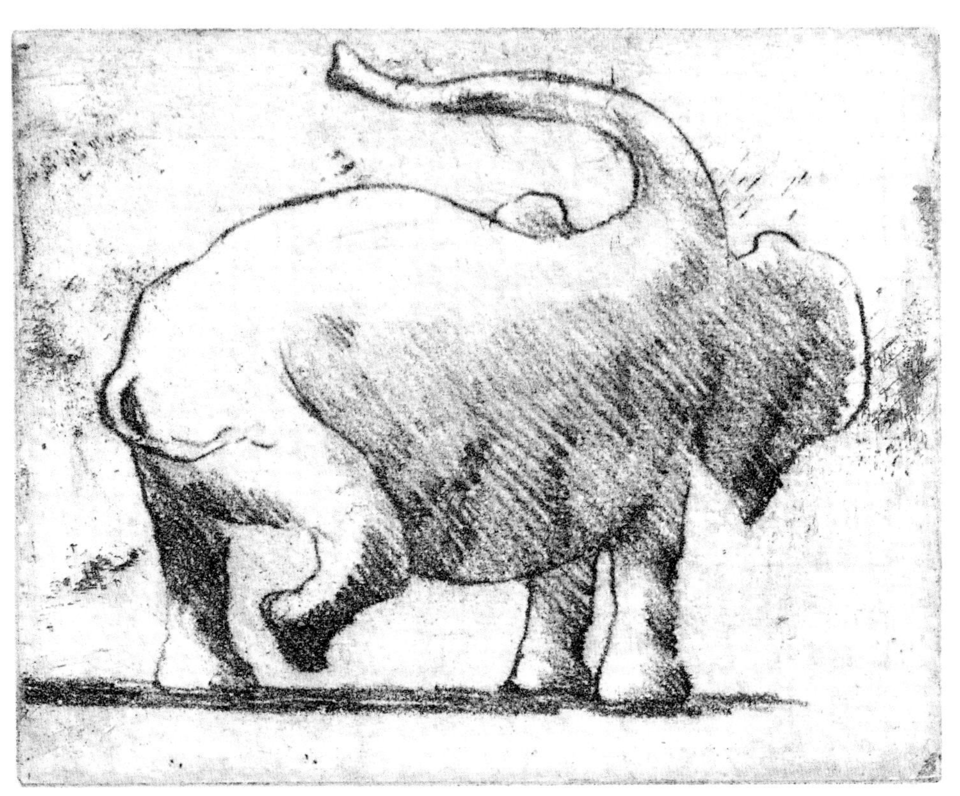

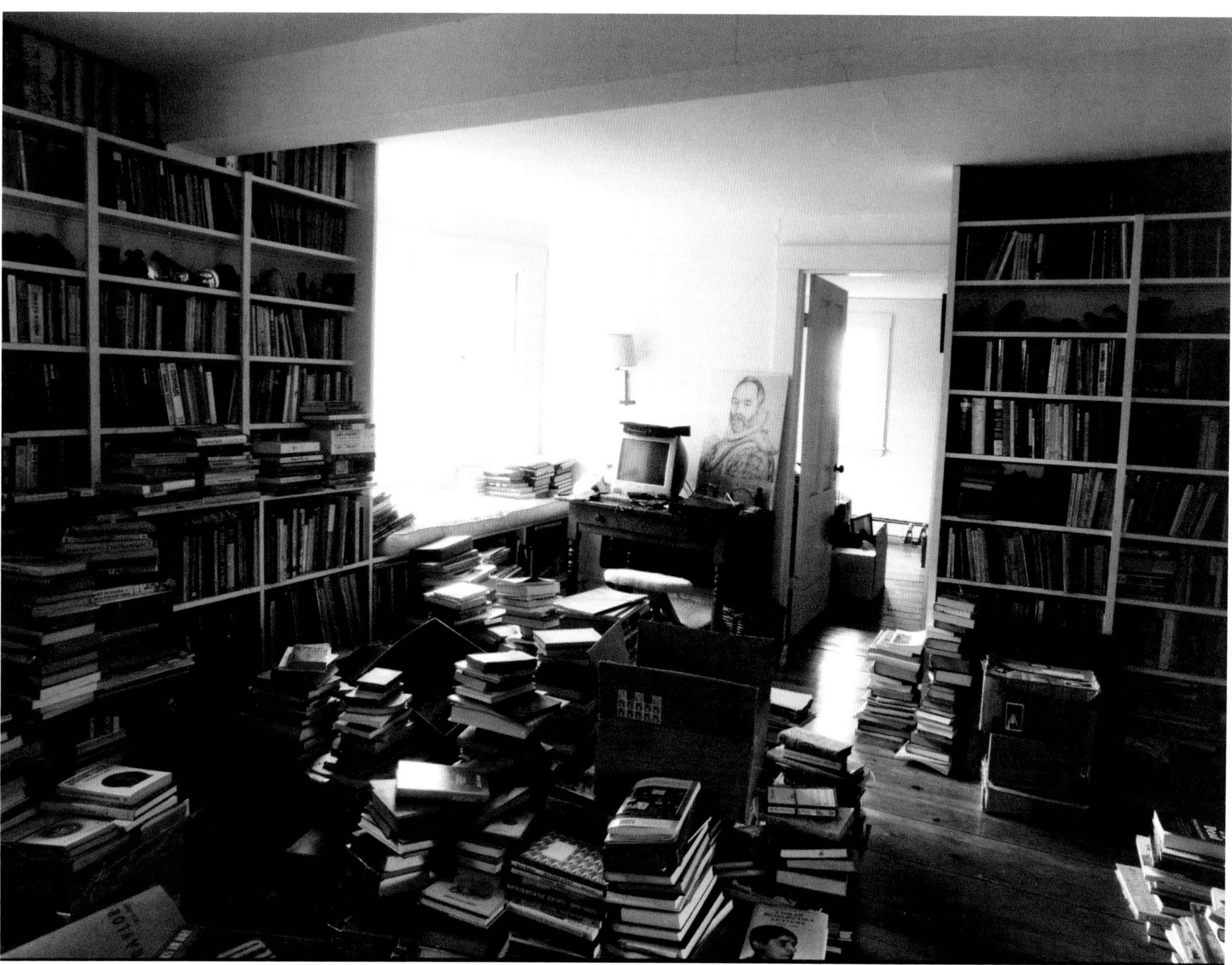

The Library

Beyond the studio, down a small hallway at the back of the second floor, was the library. In fact, this room might be described as the "book-sorting room." From here Edward eventually disbursed the newest arrivals to their appropriate places in other rooms. When he bought the house, Edward removed a wall between two small rooms to create what would become the library. He installed bookshelves and began to fill them with books. With an estimated 25,000 books in his overall collection, he had an acute storage problem. The library's floor began to sag from the weight of the books. Eventually the accumulation outgrew the house. Edward began to shelve books in his weatherized barn. Despite the apparent clutter, Edward usually knew where to find a particular work—there was a real organization to the seeming chaos.

Since his earliest years of reading he had had the habit of noting at the front of a book the date he began reading it and the date he finished. Many of his favorites contain a column of dated entries, recording subsequent readings. He was a voracious reader and often spoke of the writers he most enjoyed—Jane Austen, Lady Murasaki, Anthony Trollope, the "Lucia" books of E. F. Benson. In the last years of his life he had begun to read, with considerable enthusiasm, the complete works of Carl Jung. Japanese literature was a particular favorite and his library contained an extensive collection. He also had a fine selection of art books. His friends benefited from being able to use Edward's collection as a lending library.

Adjacent to the library was a sizeable storage room that housed an extensive collection of mysteries. Edward was an avid mystery fan and had comprehensive collections of his favorite writers in the genre.

Ever curious about evolving technology, in the late 1990s Edward bought a Bondi Blue iMac. He took classes in Adobe Photoshop and Illustrator, but he quickly discovered that the techniques he had mastered with pen and ink were nearly impossible to re-create with the computer, so he rarely used it. Always open to learning and trying new interests, he took classes in calligraphy, printmaking, pottery, tile making, and watercolor. However, in one surprising instance he stopped himself: oil painting. He would not paint in oils.

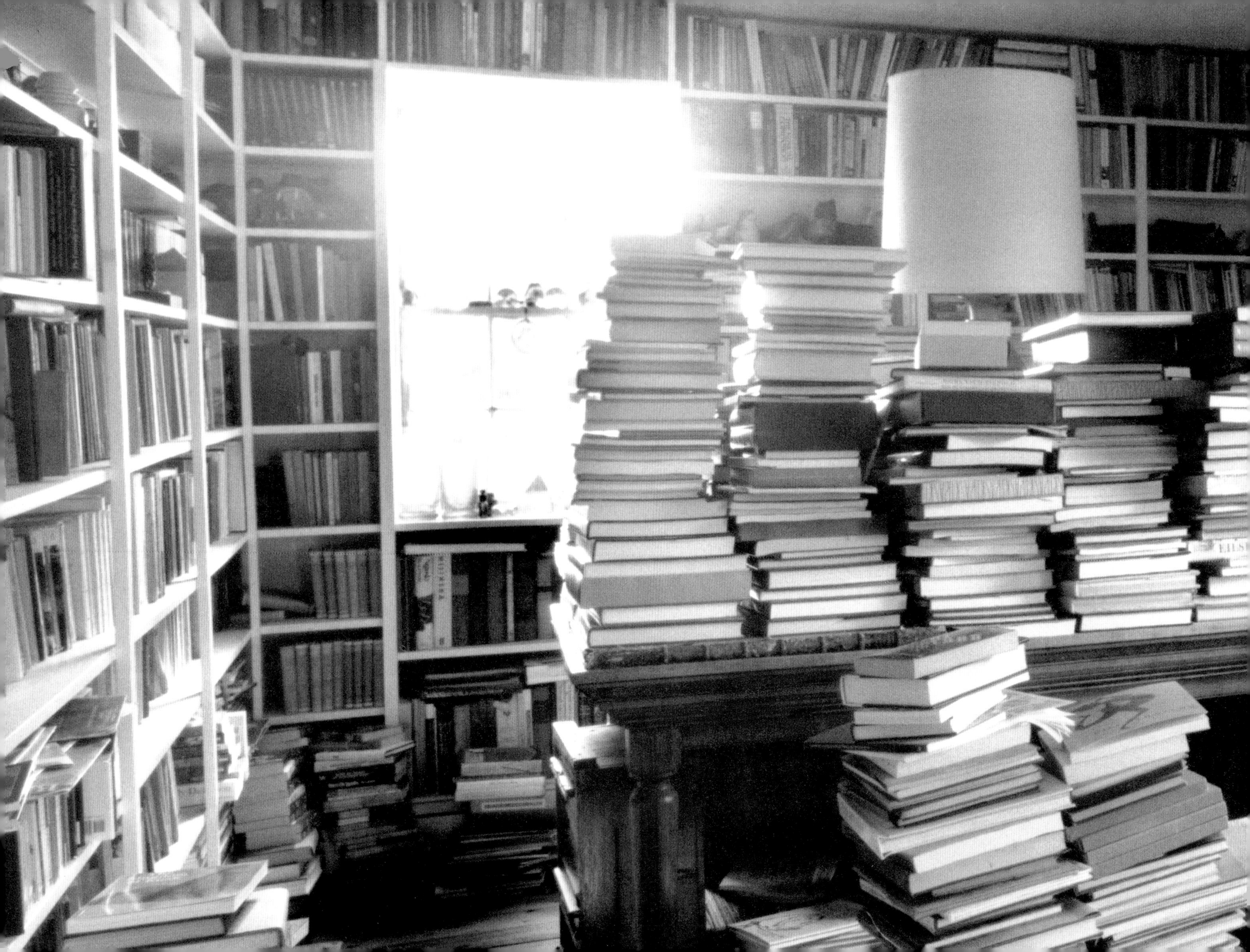

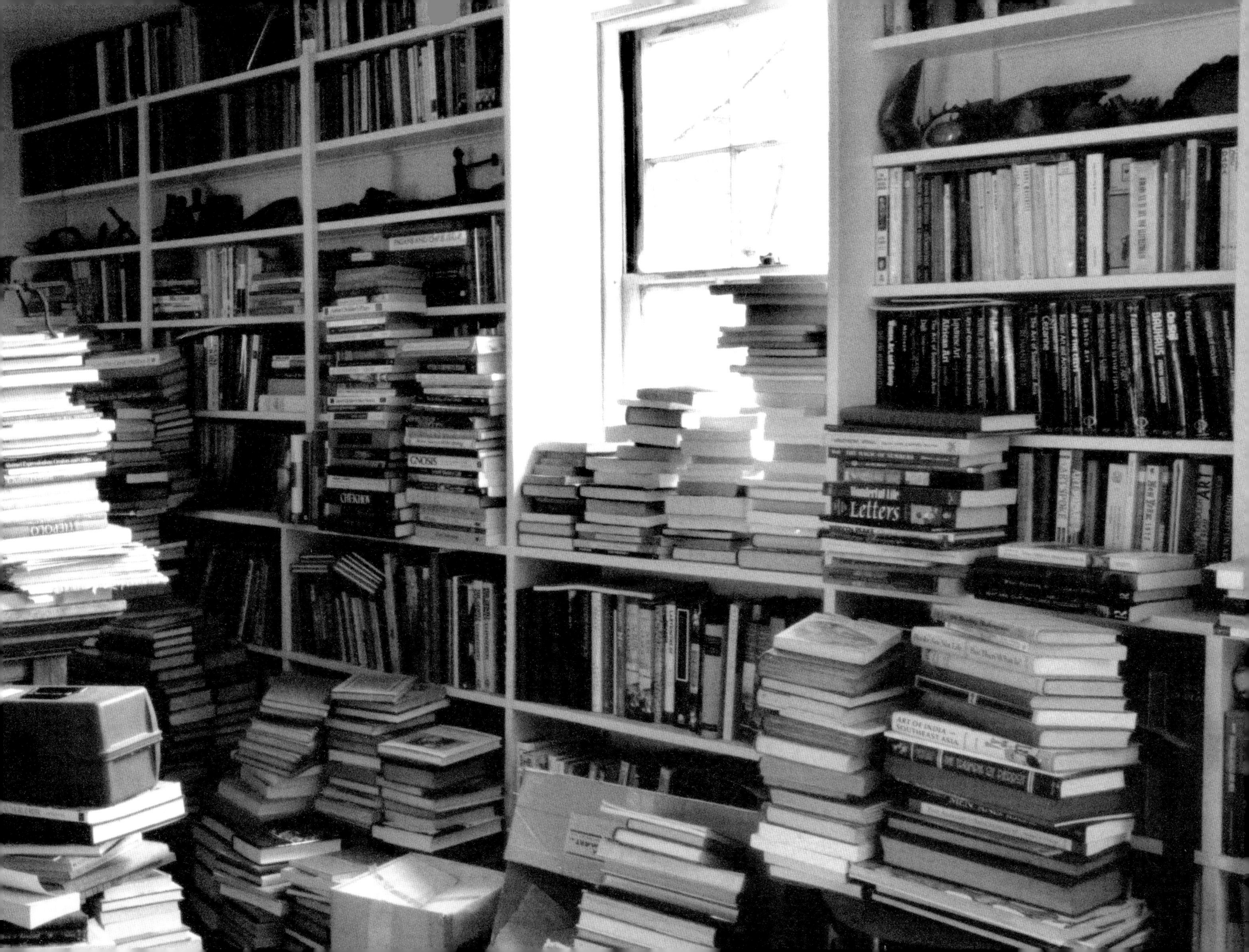
GNOSIS
CHEKHOV
Letters
BAUHAUS
ART OF INDIA — SOUTHEAST ASIA

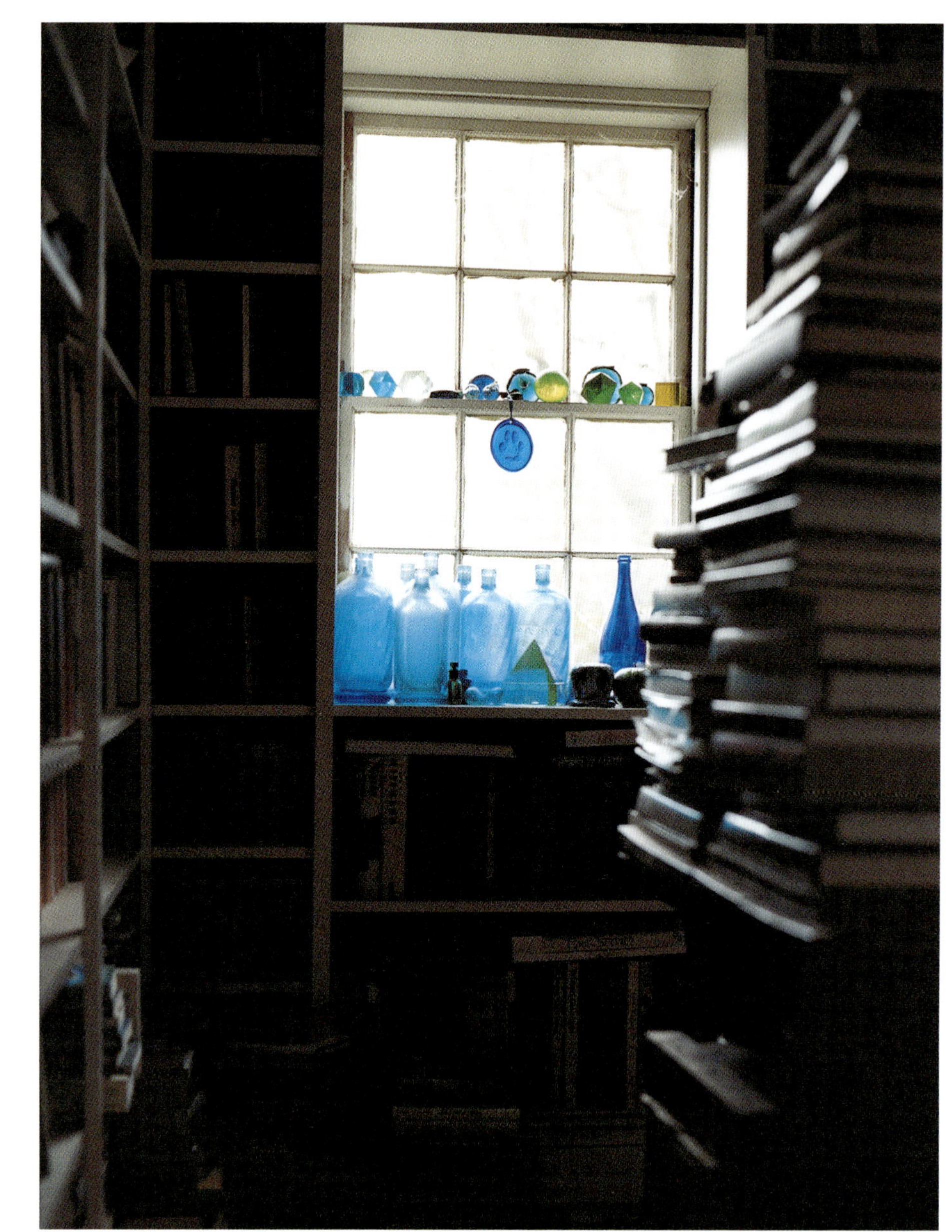

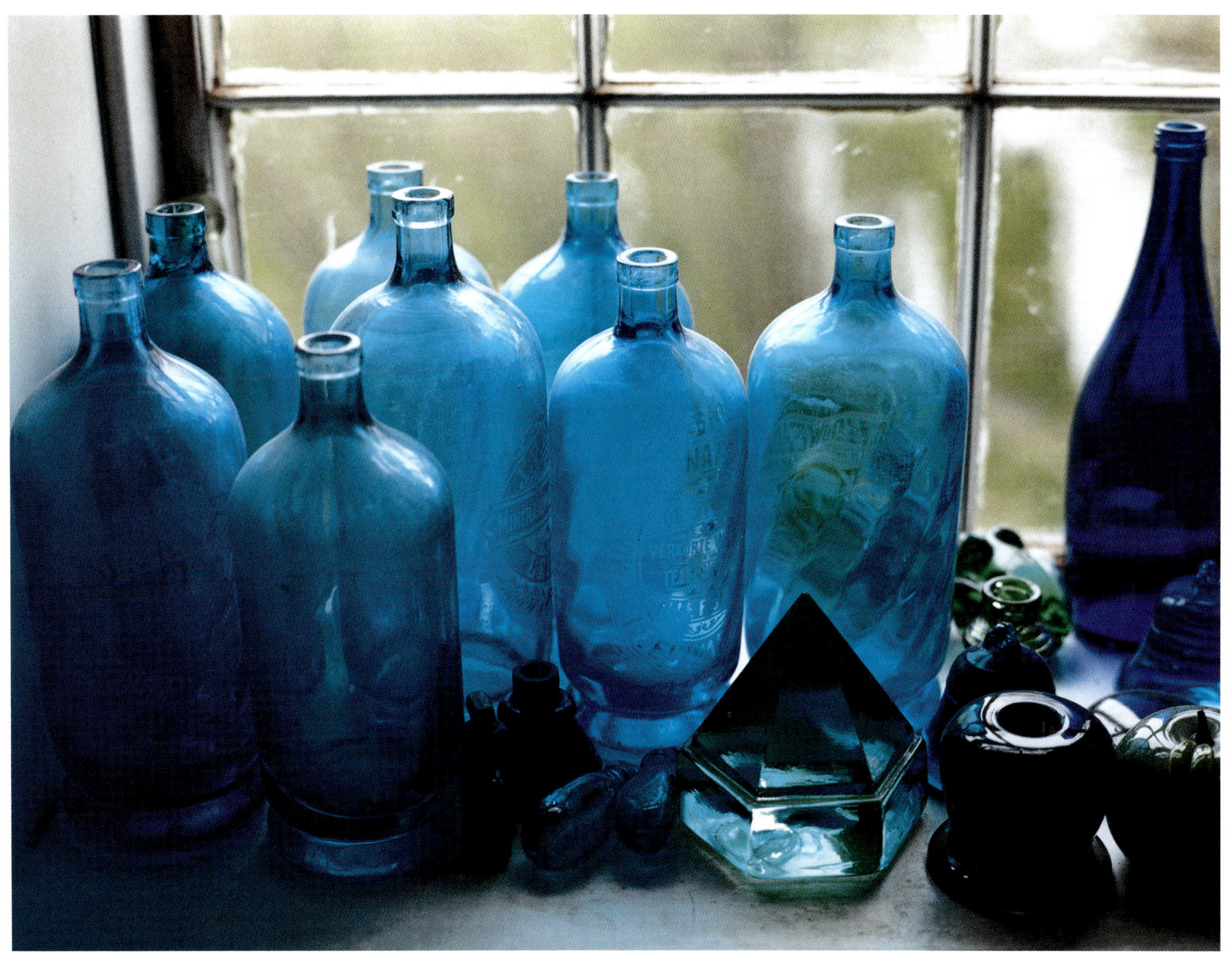

The family was baffled: though their oldest heirloom,
it was made of wax and of no value to anyone else.

—Edward Gorey, from *The Other Statue*

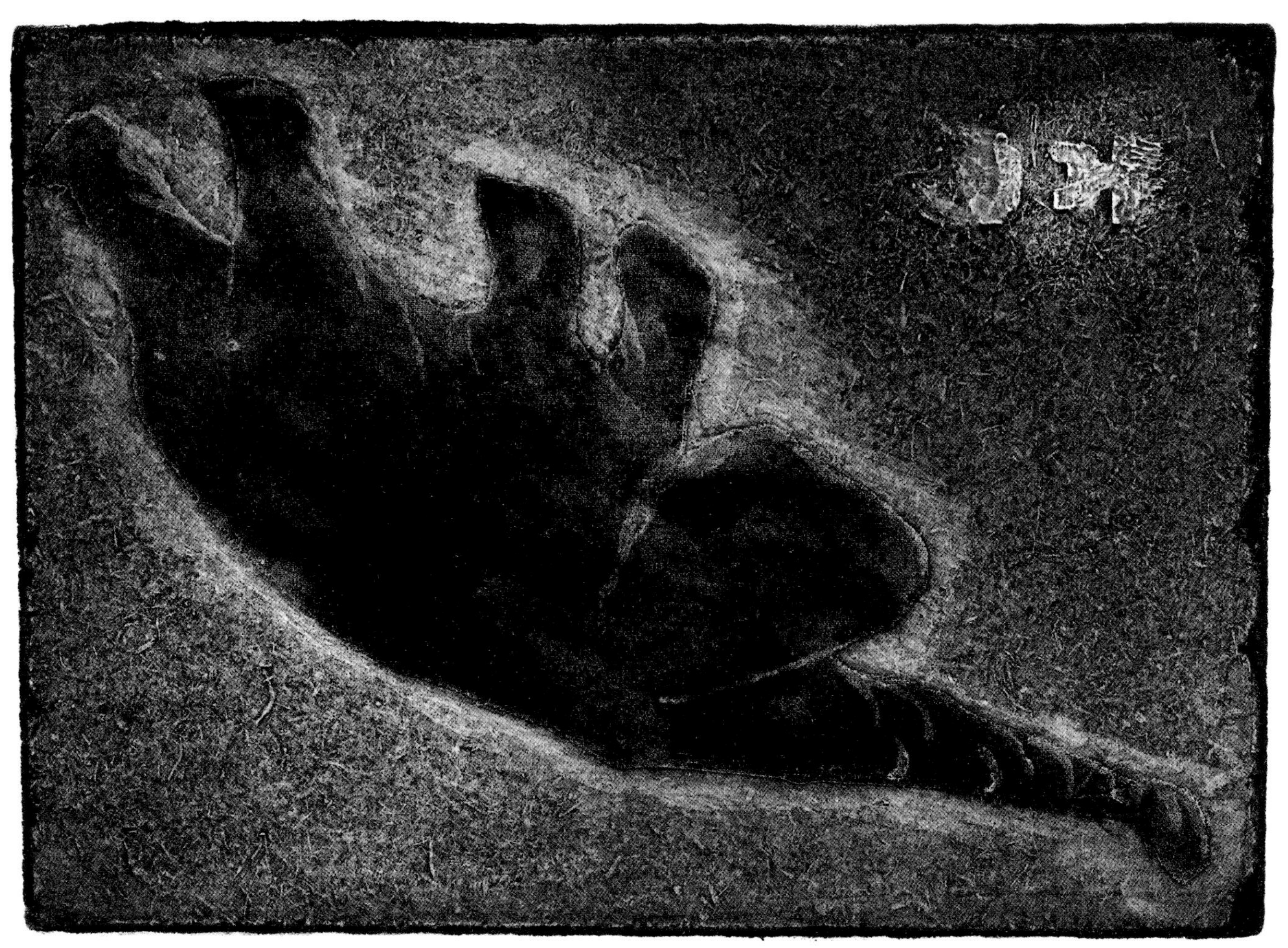

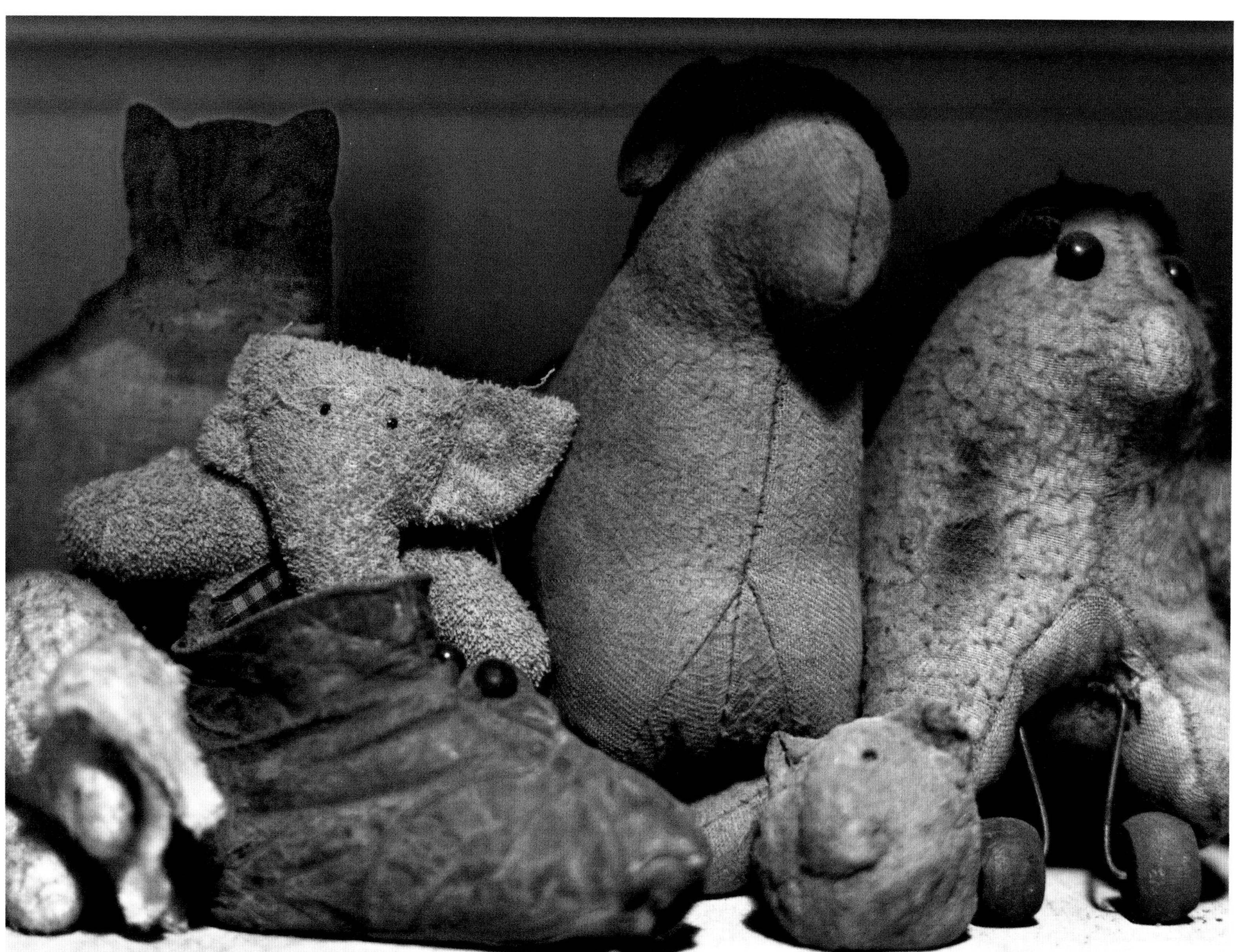

The Alcove

Passing back through the television room, walking toward Edward's bedroom, one came upon the alcove. This space was created during the renovations to the house. Edward added ceiling-to-floor shelves to display various collections. Hundreds of small animal figurines resided in the alcove, along with hundreds of books, including his treasured Agatha Christie novels and the works of Trollope and Austen. In many rooms, he often arranged his most treasured objects on shelves at his viewing level. In the alcove, these included his oldest stuffed animals. He preferred old, worn, stuffed animals—the more worn, the better. Among his favorites was a simple terry cloth elephant. Two shelves in the alcove contained a portion of Edward's large accumulation of elephant figures. He utilized the collection when he created his elephant etchings, sculpted elephants, hand-stuffed elephants, and included some of them in his book illustrations. He even created a few experimental elephants in needlepoint.

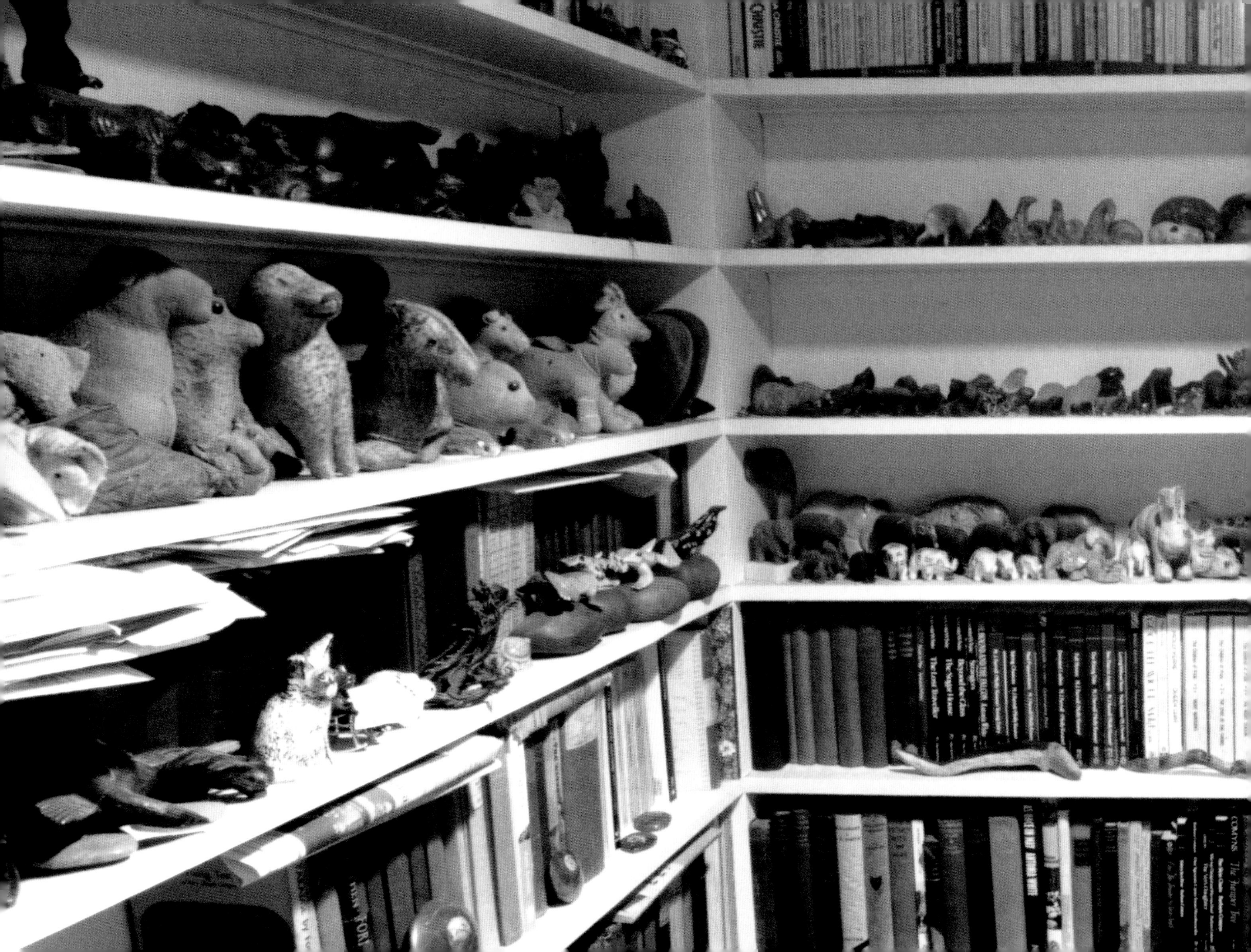
CHRISTIE
The Lost Traveller
Beyond the Glass
COMYNS The Juniper Tree

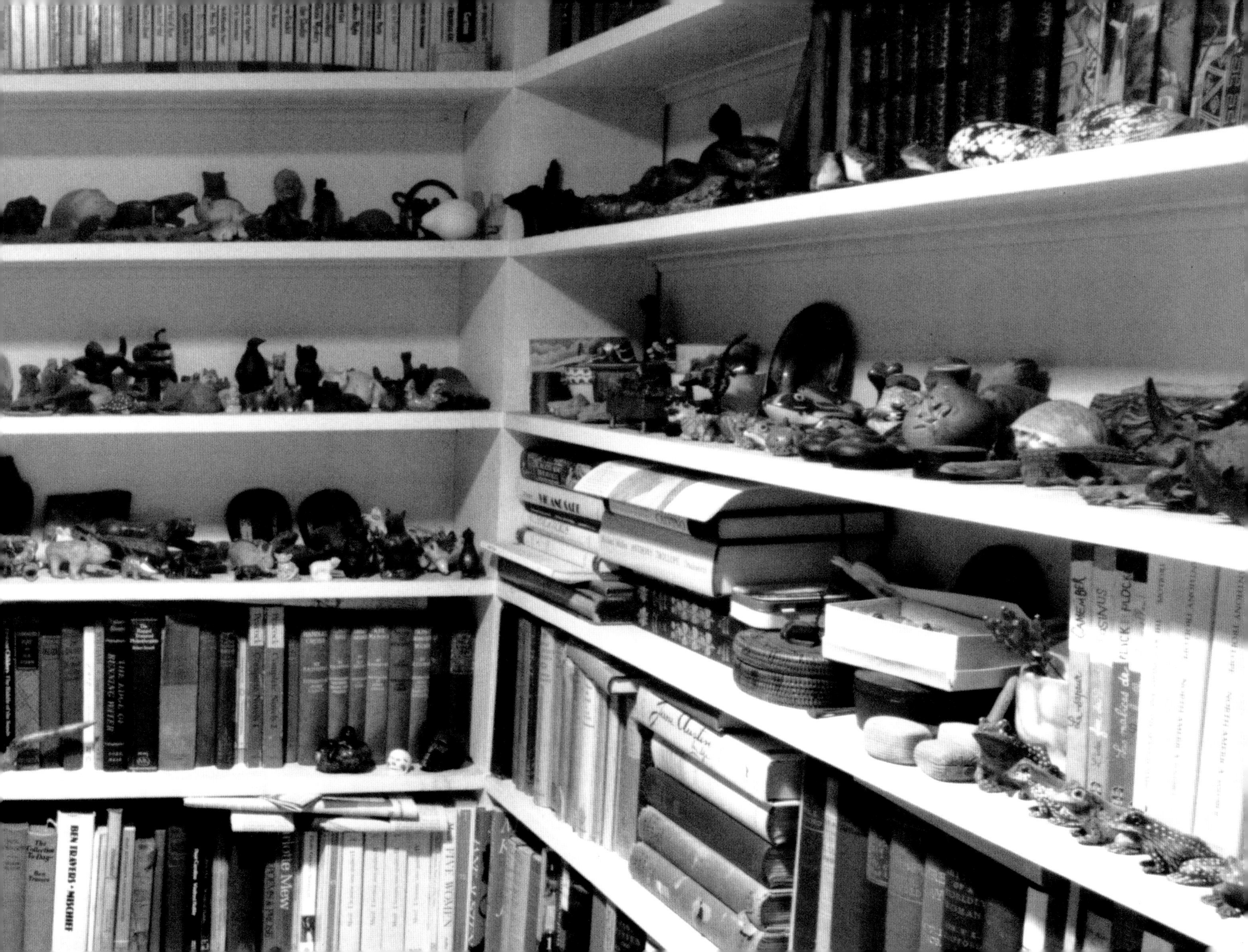
BEN TRAVERS • MISCHIEF
FIVE WOMEN
CAMEMBERT

It clears up rashes, makes mustaches
   Grow thicker rapidly;
It also numbs arthritic thumbs-
   Huzzah for Q.R.V.

He bit her ear, and said, 'My dear,
   You're simply lovely.'
She gently sighed, and then replied,
   'I bathe in Q.R.V.'

There is a balm that keeps one calm,
   And makes for scented p---;
Still furthermore, it's in *your* store-
   It's known as Q.R.V.

—Edward Gorey, from *The Universal Solvent*

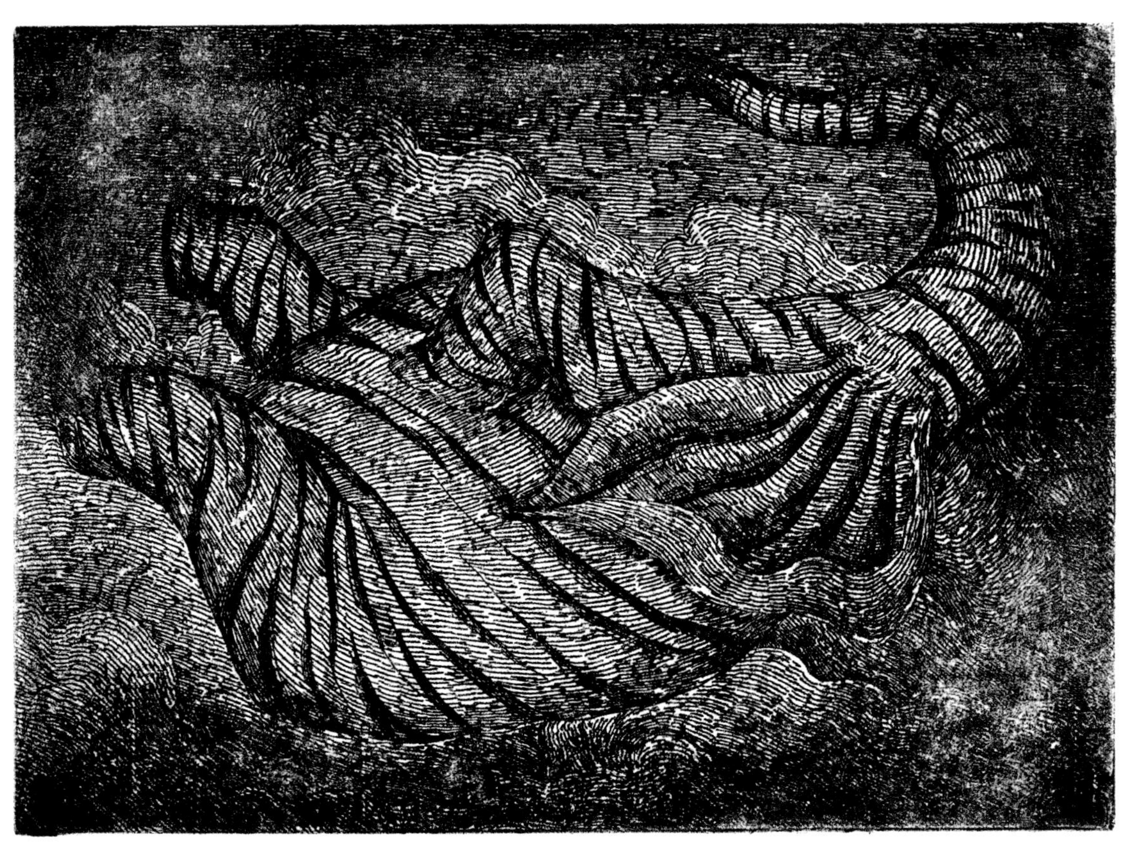

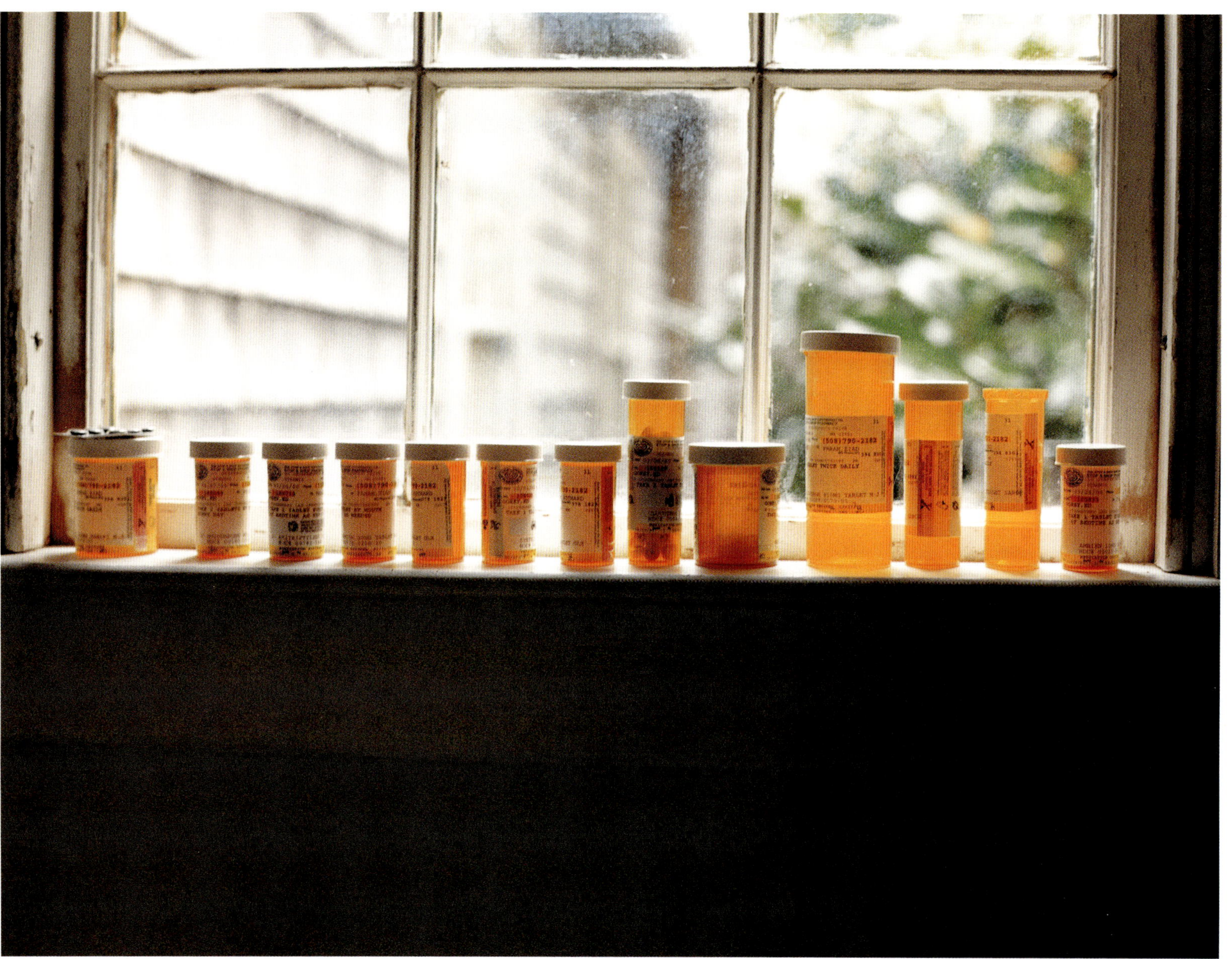
(508)790-2182
TWICE DAILY

The Bathroom

Edward wore jewelry long before it was a common occurrence to see men wearing earrings, finger rings, and neck pendants. African, Tibetan, and Indian jewelry were of particular interest to him. Some of his rings were so heavy and awkward that one had to wonder how he could function with such obstacles. In fact, some of the rings were not rings at all; they were antique gold weights that jewelers once used to measure various ounces of gold. When Edward's good friend Herbert Senn informed him of this fact, Edward refused to believe it. Inspired by the 1961 French film *Cléo from 5 to 7,* whose heroine hung her necklaces on the wall, Edward dealt with the problem of managing his ever-growing collection of jewelry by hanging his rings and pendants on wooden racks that had once held spools of thread.

Edward placed objects in every window of his house—the bathroom was no exception. He had a fear of doctors and hospitals. Near the end of his life his doctor gave him three options for dealing with his heart condition: have a pacemaker implanted, take a high dose of medication and be monitored at the hospital, or, as a temporary measure, take a smaller dose of medication at home. Edward chose the third.

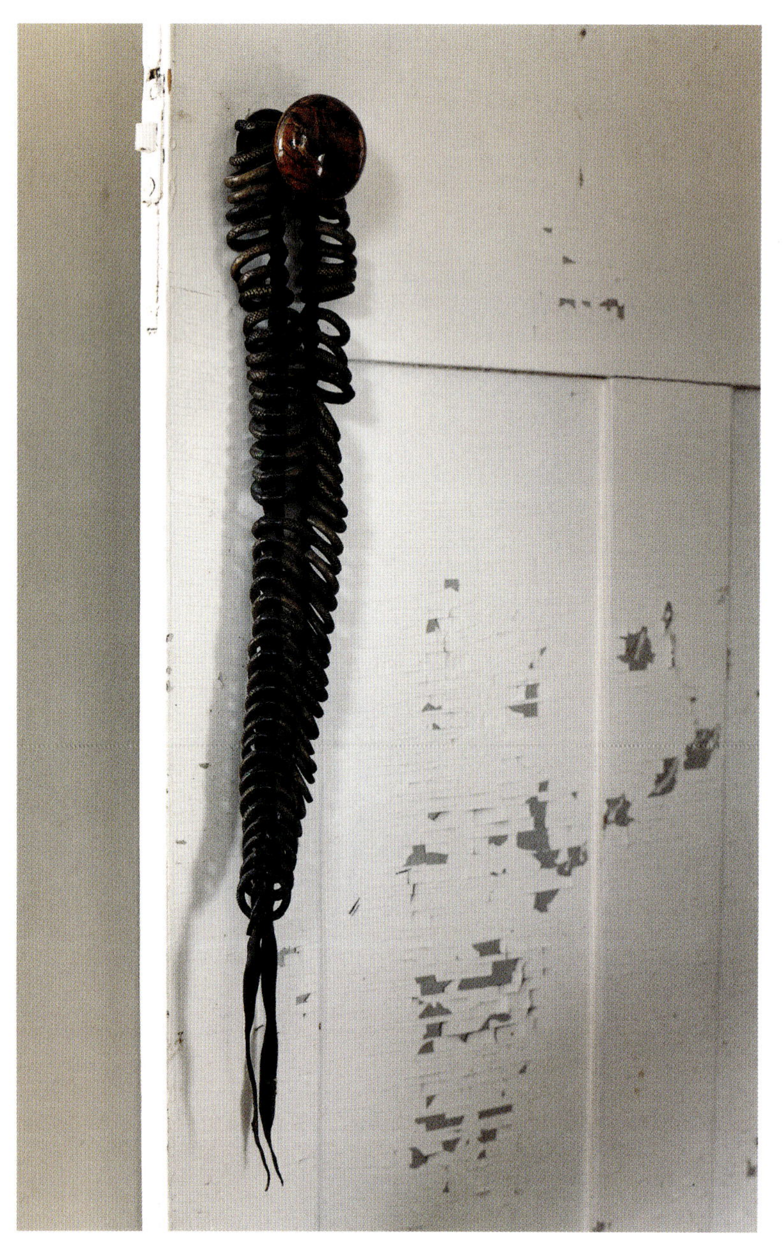

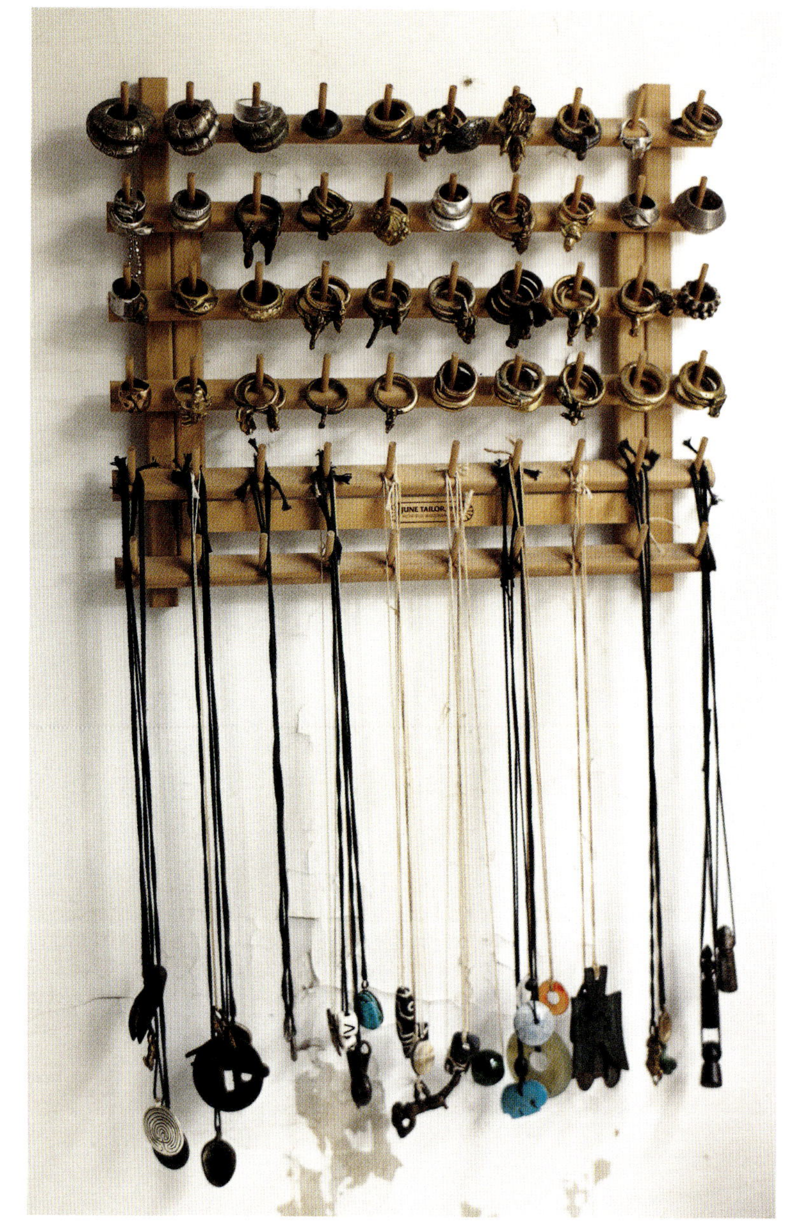
JUNE TAILOR

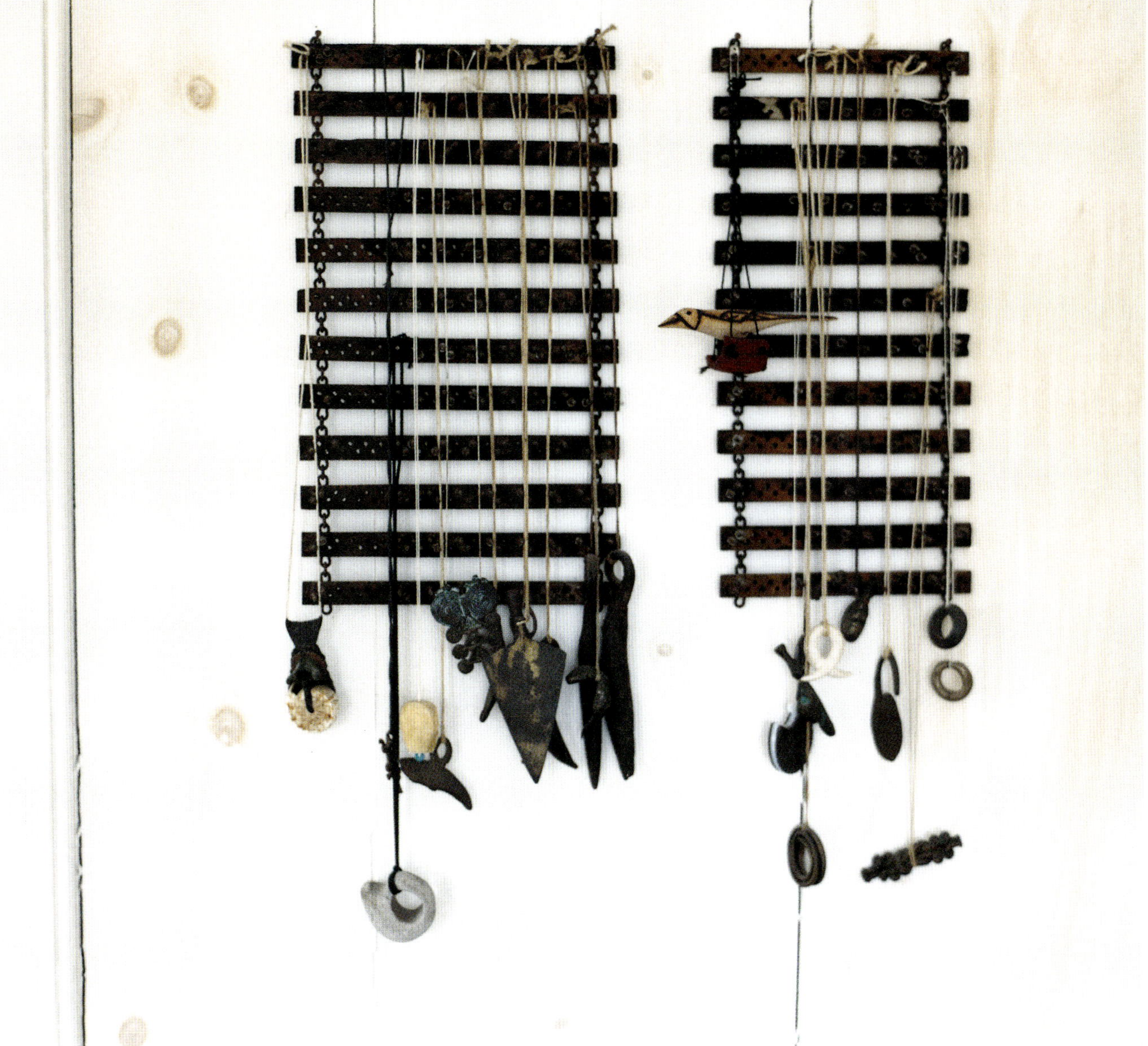

Each night father fills me with dread
When he sits on the foot of my bed:
   I'd not mind that he speaks
   In gibbers and squeaks,
But for seventeen years he's been dead.

Edward Gorey, from *The Listing Attic*

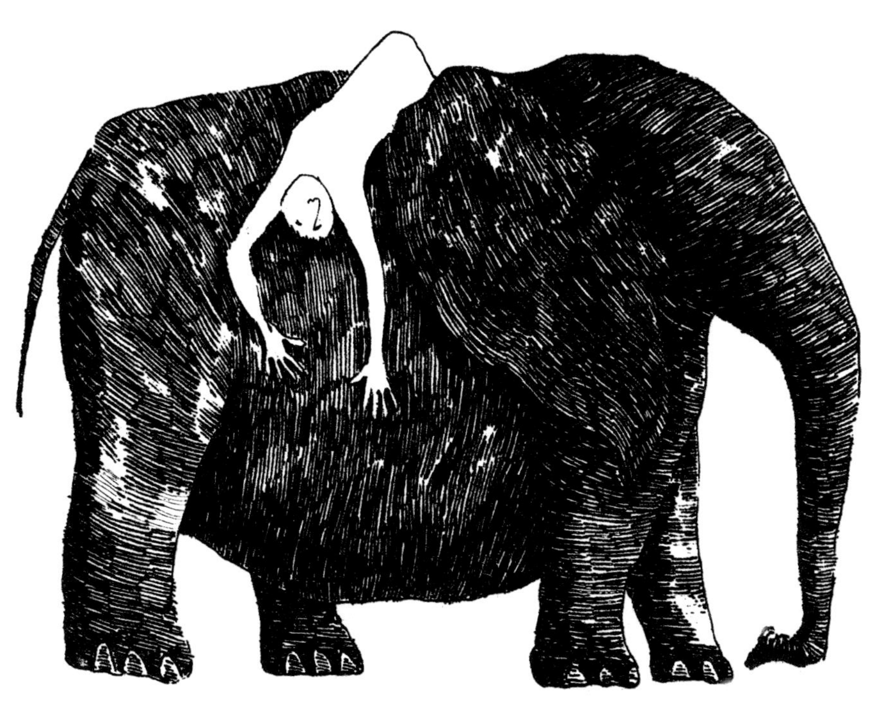

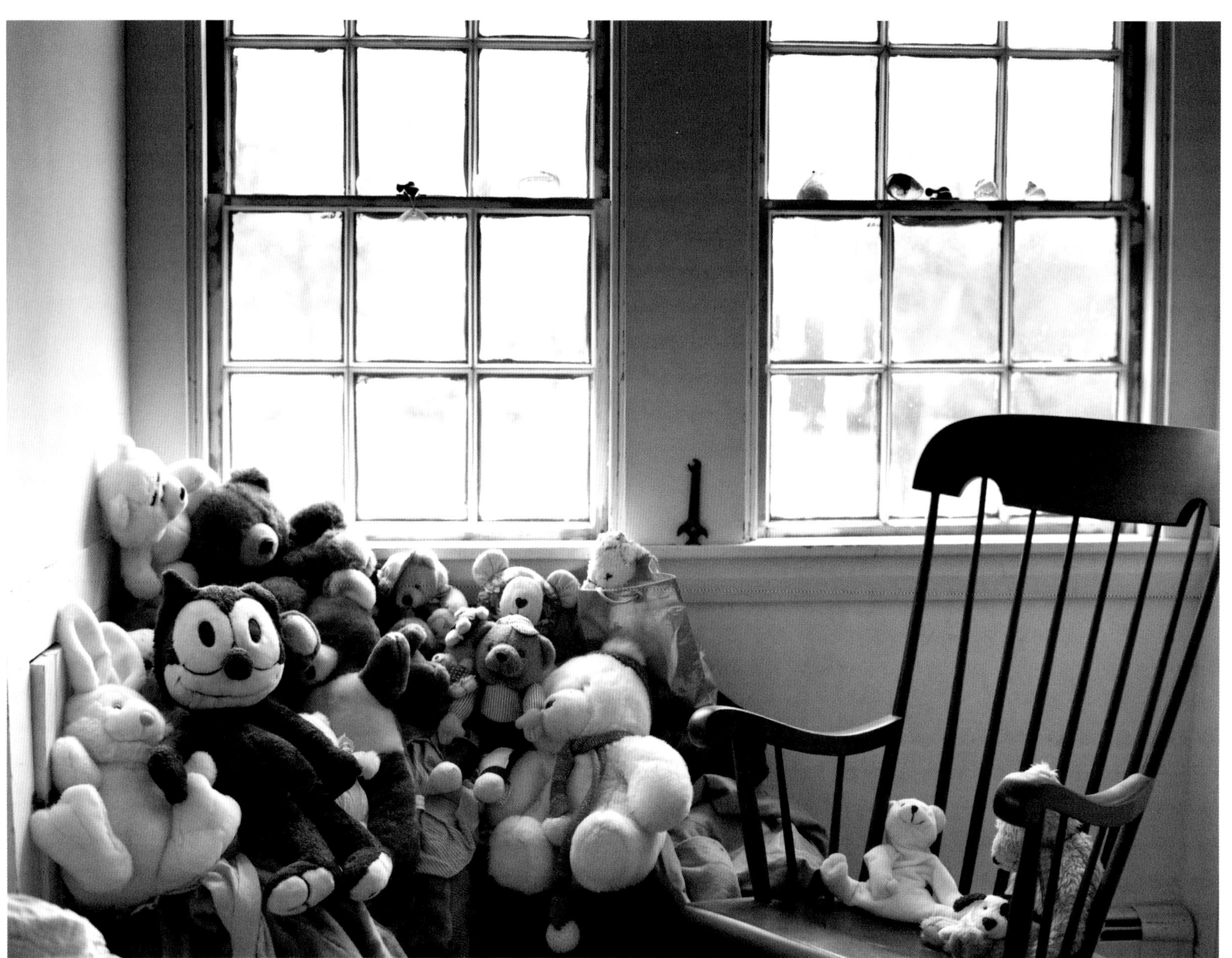

The Bedroom

Edward's bedroom was rather austere. Along the south wall was a window overlooking open meadows and several beautiful homes. Under the west window, with its sweeping view of the common green, were more stuffed animals. When people saw his interest in stuffed animals, they often gave him more as gifts. He once purchased a couple of life-size bears from a catalog; however, he couldn't keep them in the house, because the cats began to act territorially toward them.

The side chest across from his bed was covered with frog figures, elephants, and a large accumulation of ticket stubs, including every one obtained from the many times he had attended the performances of our Gorey production in Provincetown the previous summer. Over the closet door were small sculptures of a crow and a couple of hippos as well as a large iron ring holding his handmade dolls (a figbash, a frog, and a snake). The weekend after Edward's death, his "alpha" cat, Jane, spent many hours on Edward's bed.

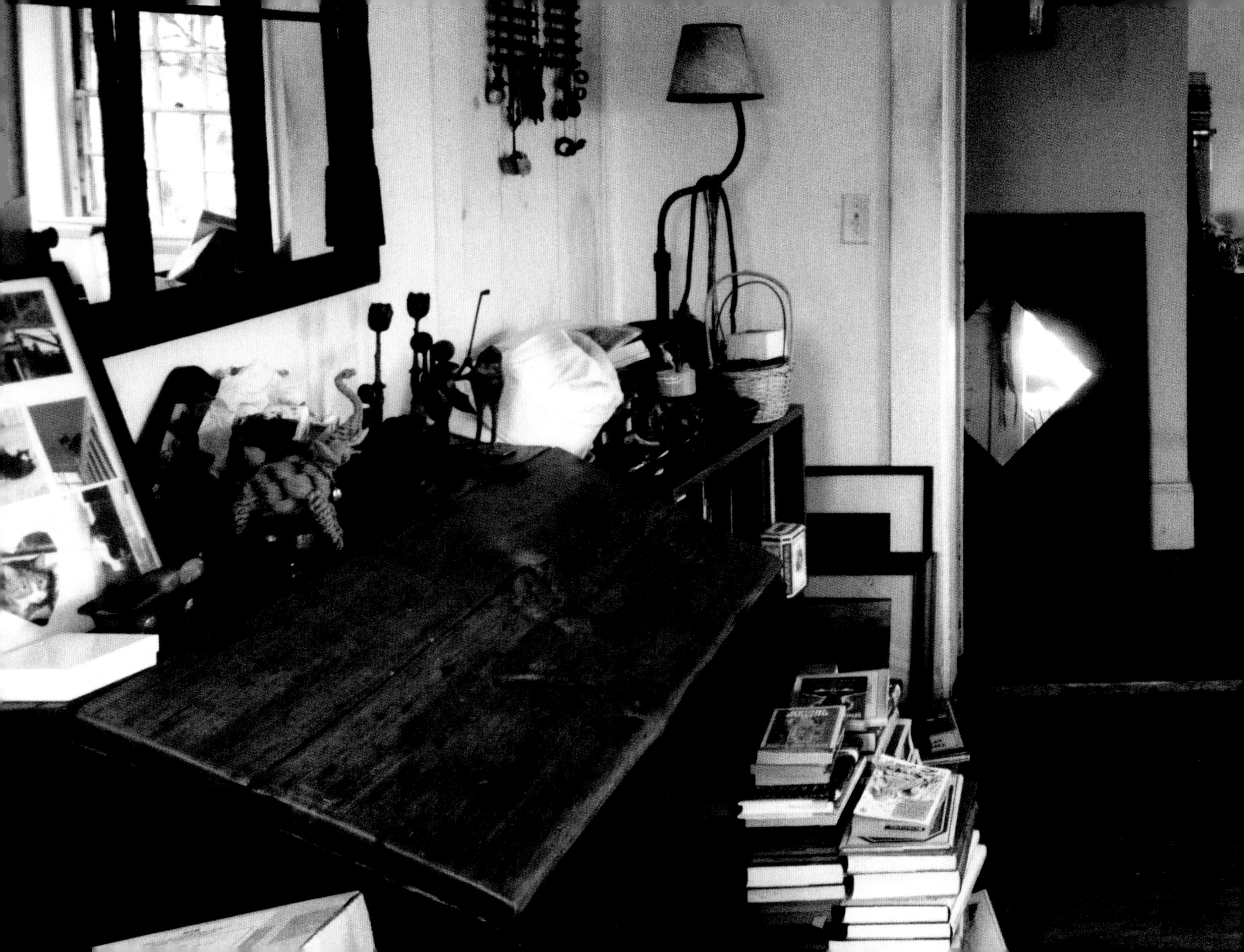

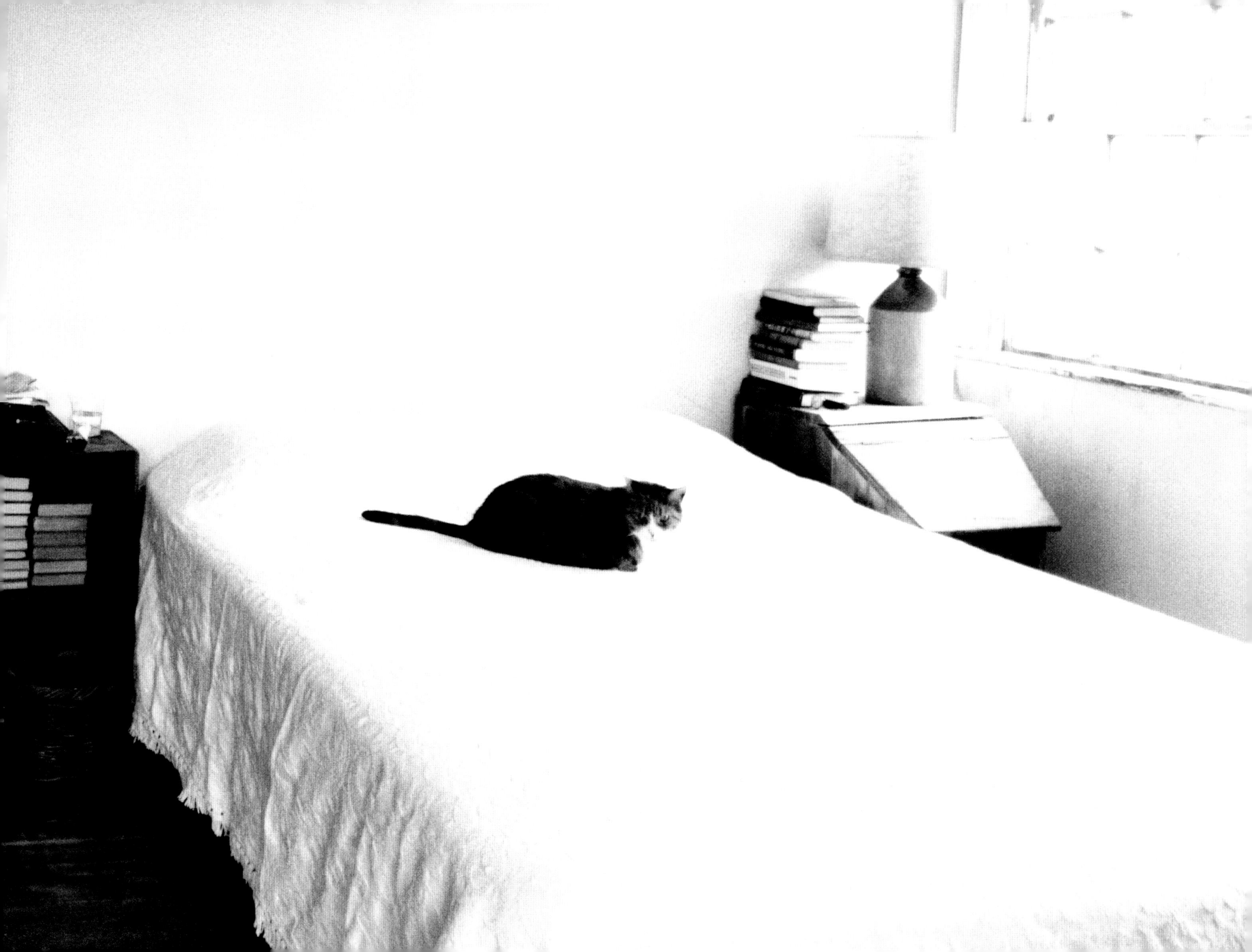

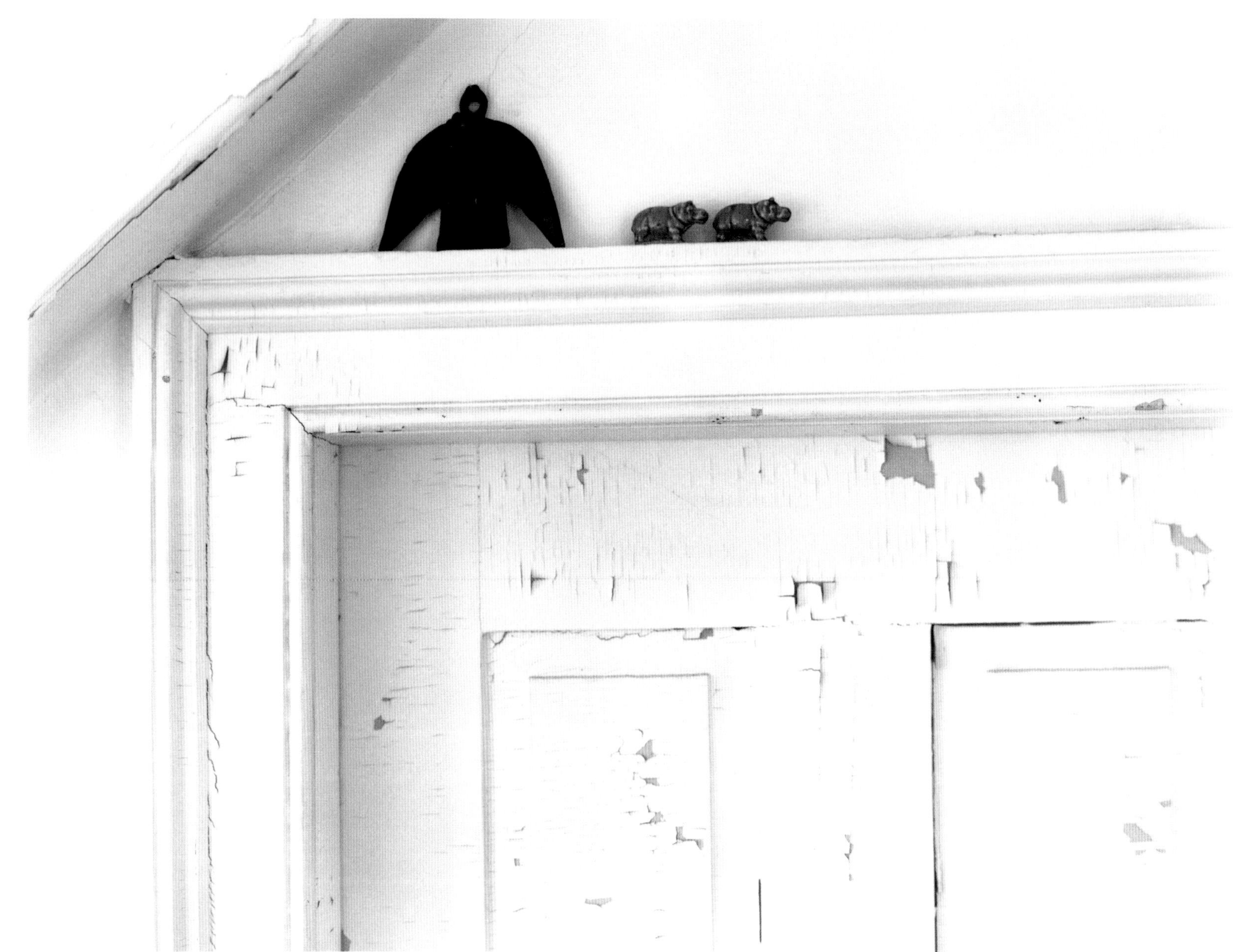

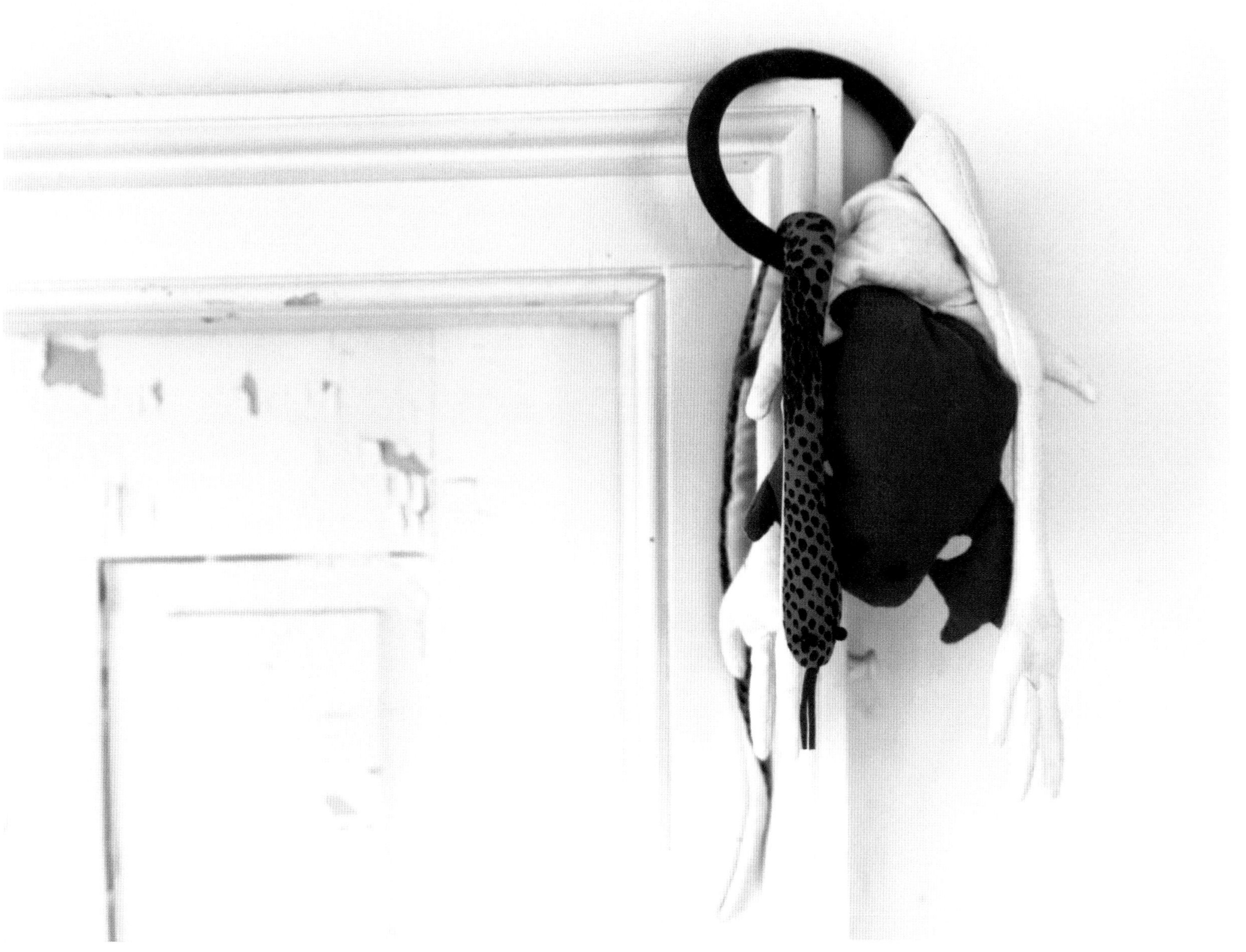

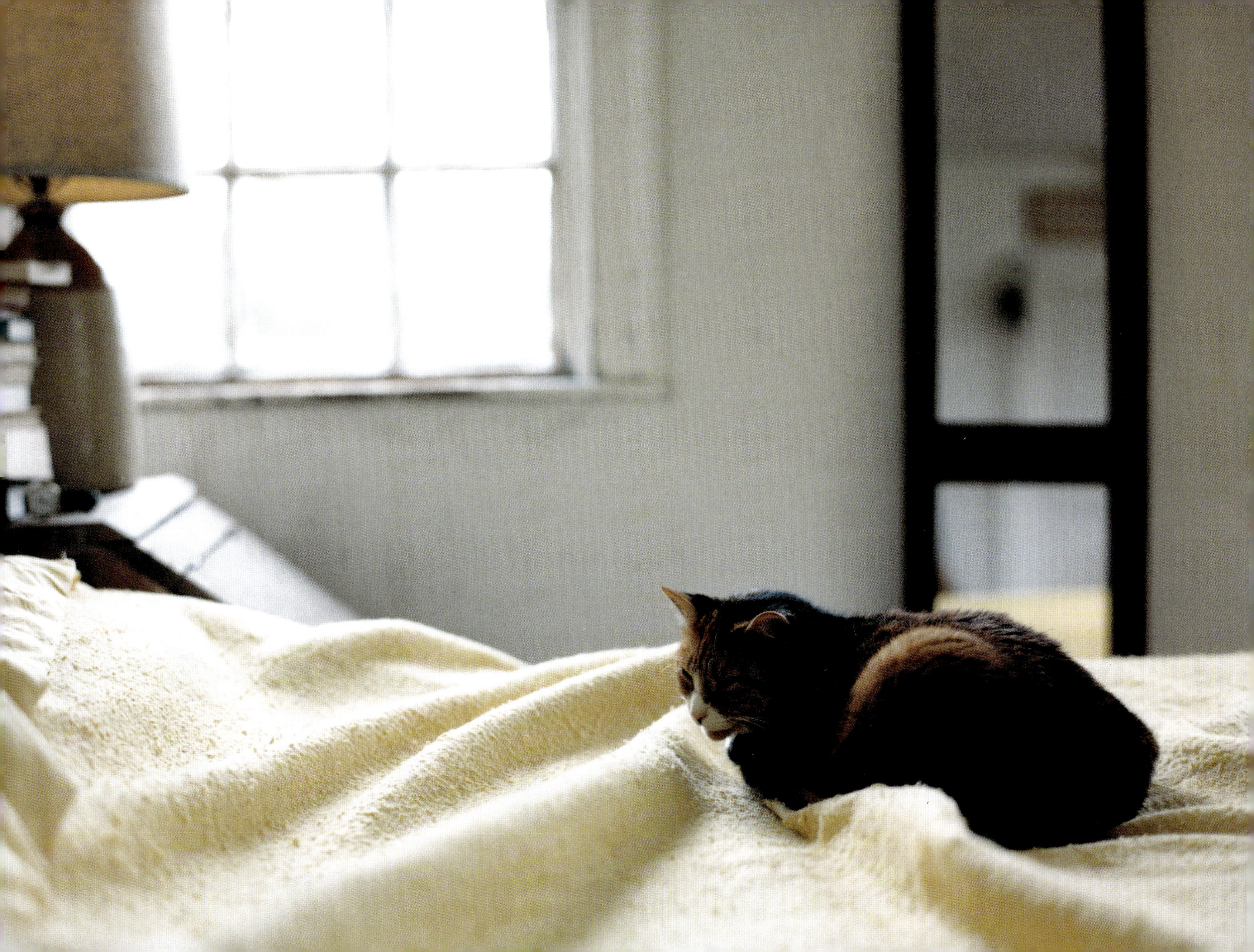

What or who is the greatest love of your life?

"Cats."

If you were to die and come back as a person or thing what do you think it would be?

"A stone."

What is your favorite journey?

"Looking out the window"

—from an interview in *Vanity Fair,* October 1997

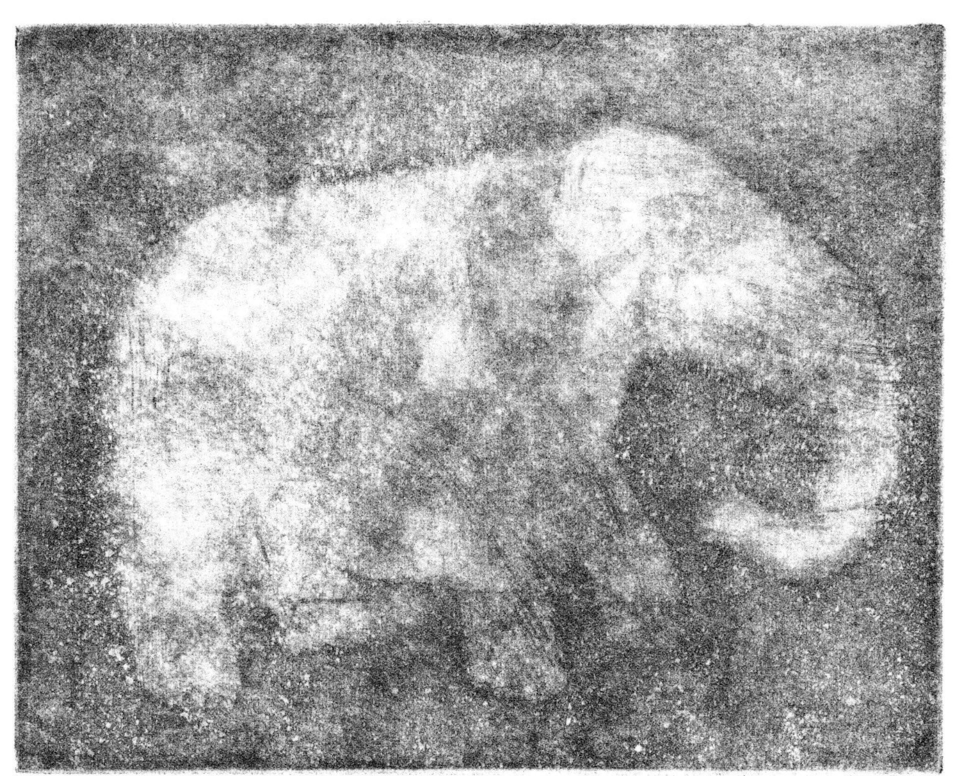

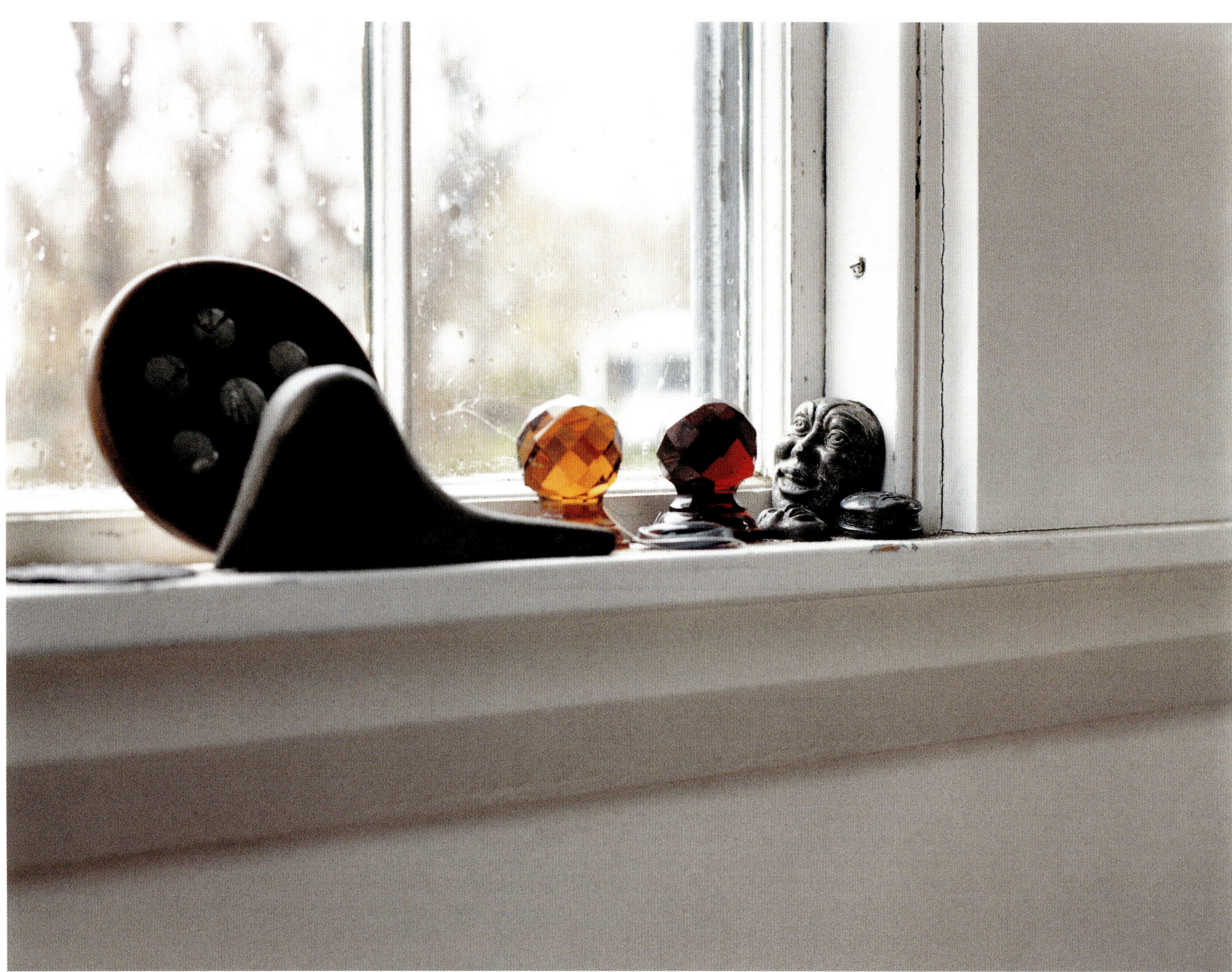

The Hidden Room

This was called "the children's room." When Edward's friends Mel and Alex stayed in the house, their daughter, Annabelle, slept in this room. The room held a large selection of children's literature as well as a couple of Edward's old fur coats, which had begun to shed from lack of care. (Edward stopped wearing his fur coats once he left New York.) Later Edward closed off the door that opened to the television room by blocking it with a bookcase filled with videotapes and CDs. While standing in the television room, a visitor to the house would probably not even be aware of this room's existence. The hidden room also housed the bust of Charles Dickens placed by Edward in the window facing the common. The bust became a trademark of Elephant House, looking out the window since Edward had moved in. A visitor to the house could not escape Mr. Dickens peering down from the second floor.

I completed photographing the house and then realized that I had not come across the bust. I found the room by locating a second door at the back of Edward's bedroom closet. As I opened the door, I felt a sense of discovery, much like coming upon the stone serpent in the tall grass on the lawn. The dusty room had a musty smell. I had to break through cobwebs to move forward. There was the bust, gazing stoically out at the Yarmouthport Common. Due to the rainy weather and the late hour of the afternoon, the bust was clearly reflected in the window. I lifted my camera and took my shot. Weeks later, when I printed the photograph, I was taken aback. Looking at the image, I could swear that I was seeing Edward's reflection in the glass. But I thought that maybe I was letting my imagination run away with me—perhaps I *wanted* to see Edward's face in the window. Yet when I showed the photograph to Edward's friends and family, they also felt they saw him clearly in the reflection. Perhaps Edward was leaving us something as mysterious as the message written on the card found in the empty tea urn at the end of *The Object Lesson*—the single word "farewell."

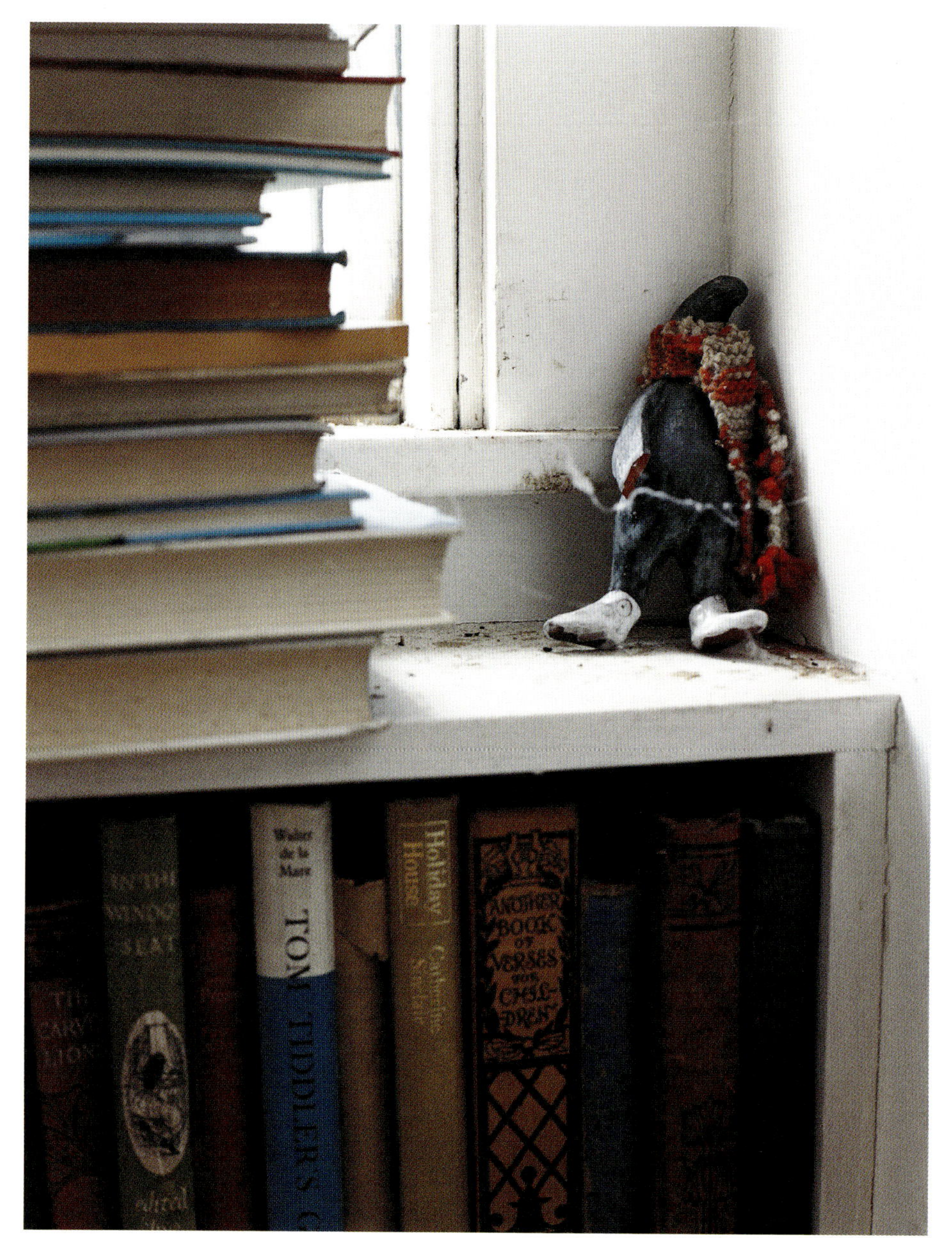
Walter de la Mare
TOM TIDDLER'S
Holiday House
ANOTHER BOOK OF VERSES FOR CHIL-DREN

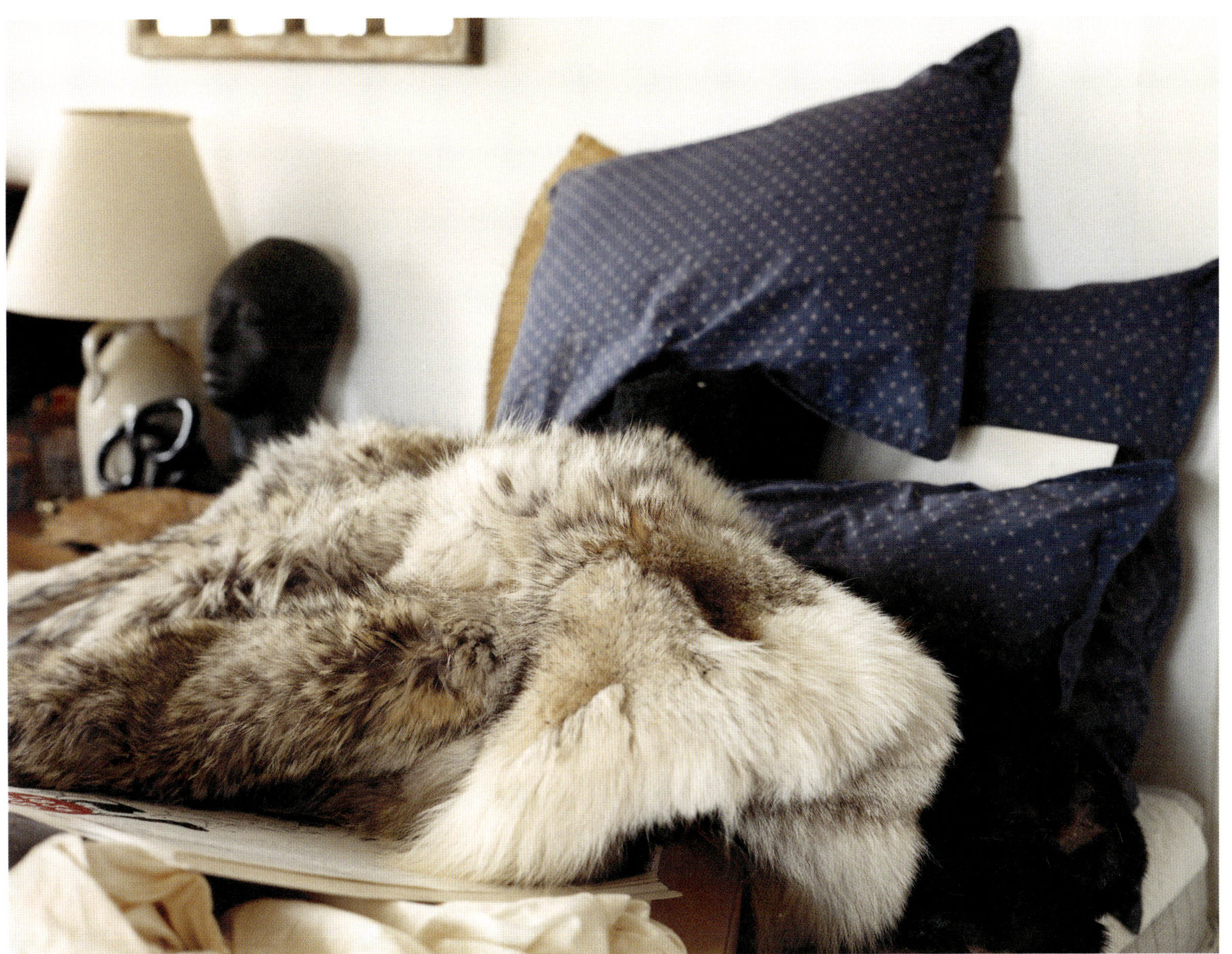

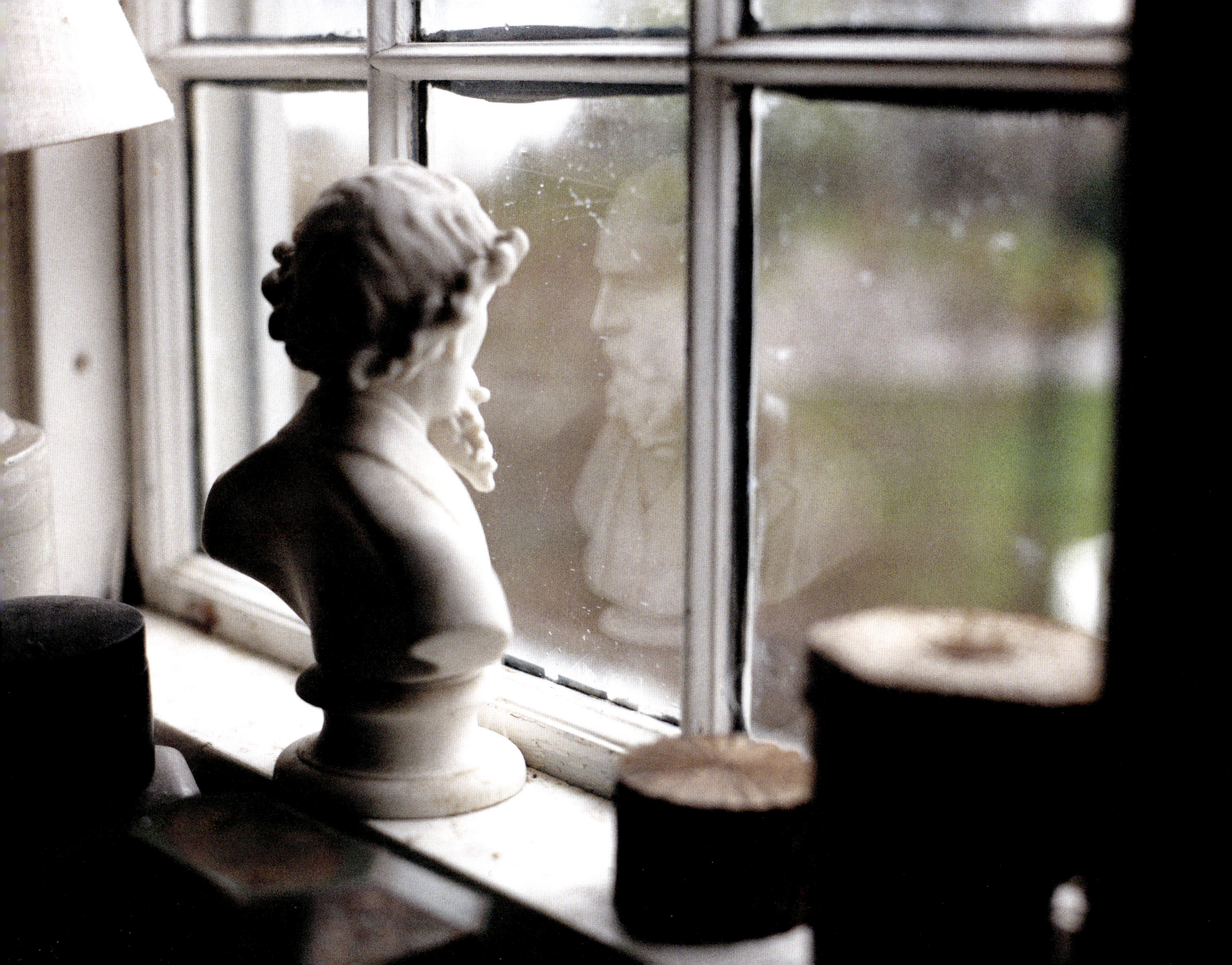

In making this book become a reality I received the generous help of Rick Jones, Skee, Roy, and Ken Morton, Eleanor Garvey, Mel and Alex Schierman, Helen Pond and Herbert Senn, Jack Braginton-Smith, Emily Trevor, and especially Andreas Brown of the Gotham Book Mart. All of their personal remembrances of Edward helped to give this book life.

My thanks to the Trustees of the Estate of Edward Gorey for their cooperation in this effort. Rebecca Schroeder, Director and Curator of The Edward Gorey House, helped with historical information on the house. I thank John Wulp for beginning my journey with Edward. Eric Etheridge and Kate Browne have provided encouragement and much-appreciated assistance. The staff of the Gotham Book Mart has been a constant source of support. I am grateful to Katie Burke at Pomegranate for her trust. I would especially like to thank Sam Shahid for his taste and elegance in the design of this book, and his art director, Matthew Kraus, for his inspiration.

Finally, I thank my brothers and sisters for their constant love and support, especially Micki and Michelle for their faith and my brother Michael for the gift of a camera.

Kevin McDermott

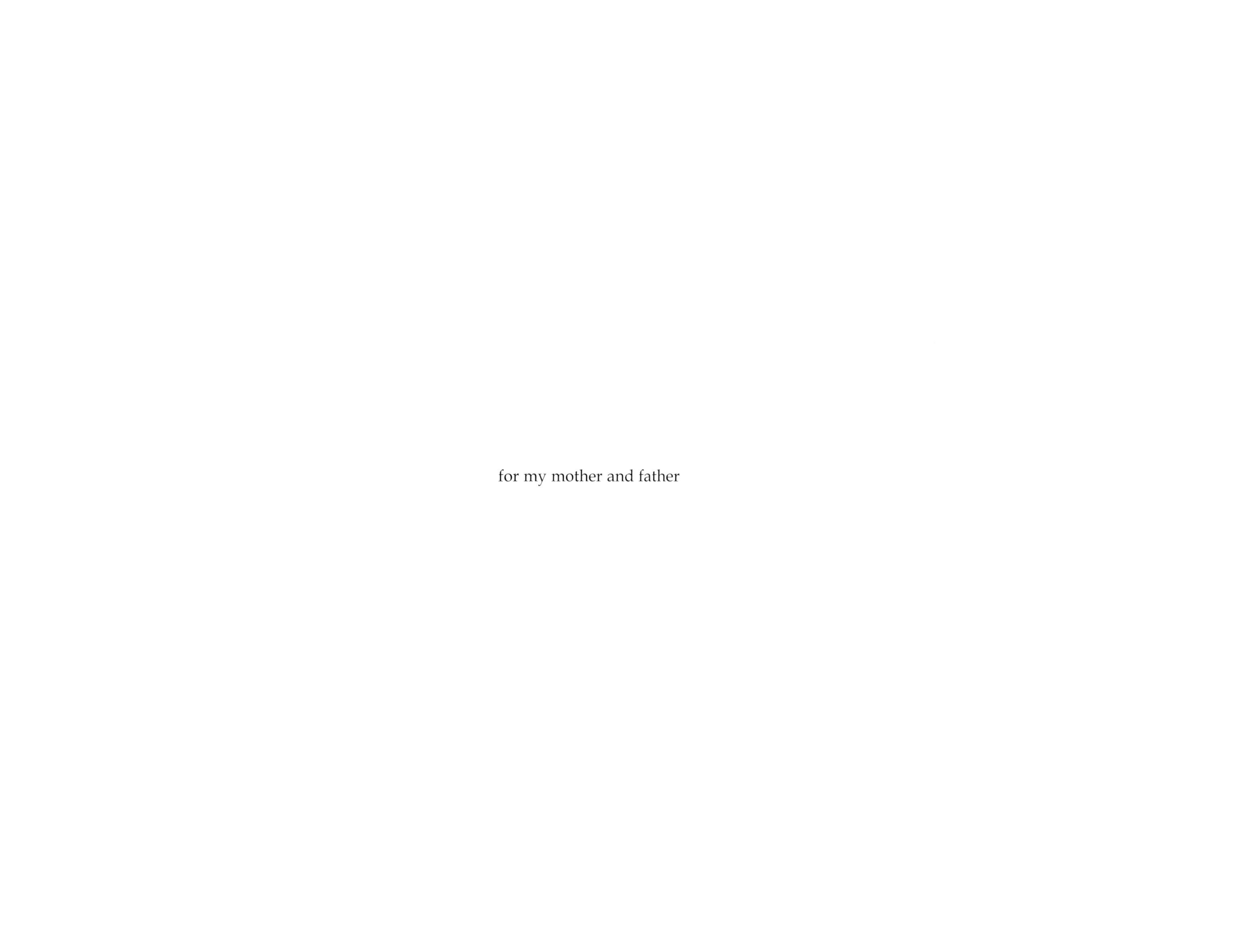
for my mother and father

The elephant images that appear throughout this book were created by Edward Gorey in 1985. They are part of a limited edition series of hand-pulled etchings and collagraphs printed at the atelier of Emily Trevor in Brewster, Massachusetts, and published by the Gotham Book Mart & Gallery, Inc., New York, New York. In addition, *Self-portrait with Elephant*, a pen and ink drawing, c. 1985, appears before "The Studio." Two sheets of elephant rubber stamp doodles and sketches created by Edward c. 1995 appear as the endpapers of this book.

Pomegranate Communications, Inc. 105 SE 18th Ave., Portland, OR 97214
800-227-1428 pomegranate.com
sales@pomegranate.com

Library of Congress Cataloging-in-Publication Data

McDermott, Kevin, 1964-
Elephant house : or, the home of Edward Gorey / photographs and text by Kevin McDermott.
p. cm.
ISBN 978-0-7649-2495-8 (alk. paper)
1. Gorey, Edward, 1925—Homes and haunts—Massachusetts—Yarmouth Port—Pictorial works. 2. Elephants in art. I. Title

NX512.G67M33 2003
700'.92—dc21
2003042875

Item No. A679
Printed in China
34 33 32 31 30 29 28 27 26 25 14 13 12 11 10 9 8 7 6 5

Design by Sam Shahid & Company

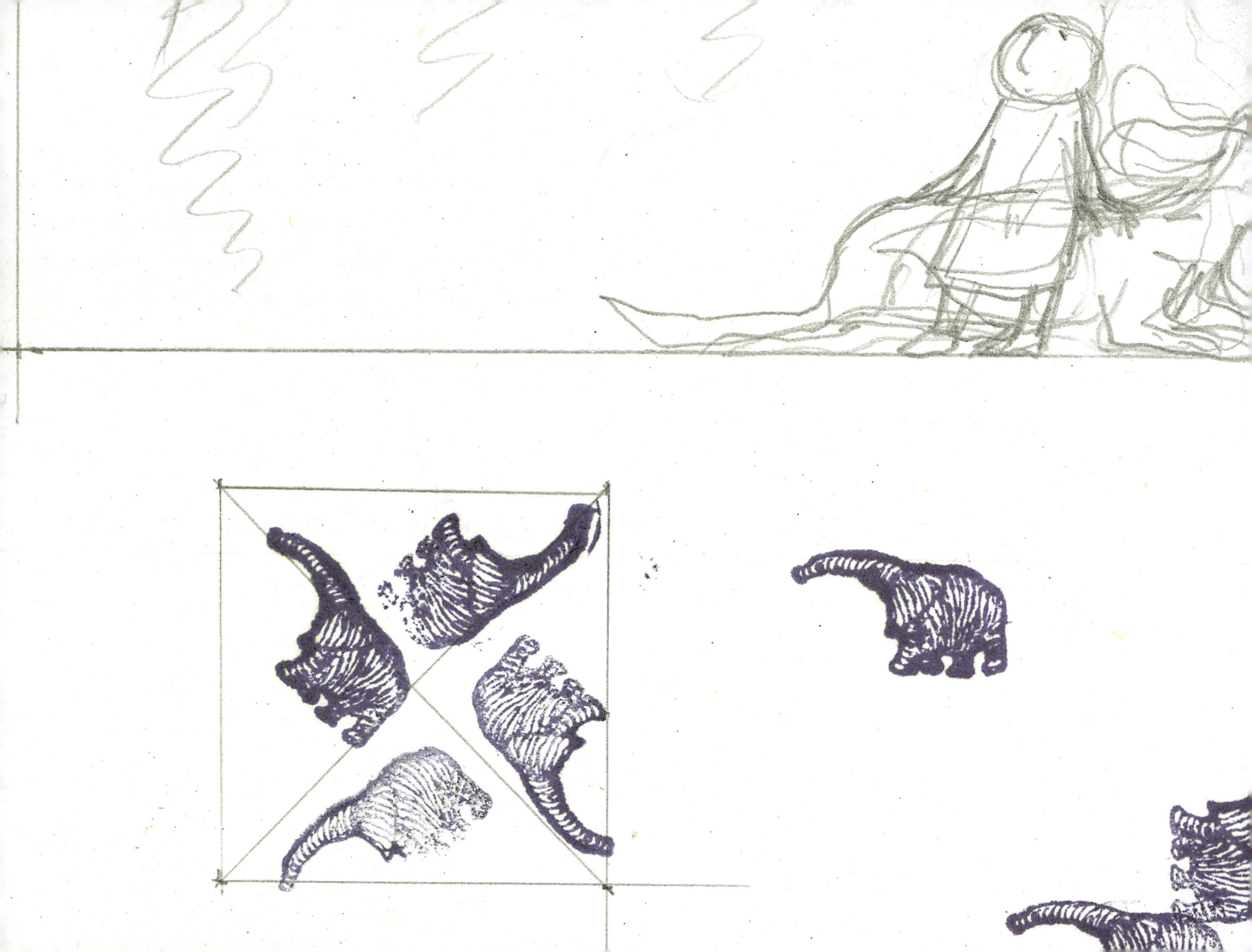